# *The* CAREER RESEARCH PROJECT

DR. DENISE C. LAGOS

D1529967

**Kendall Hunt**
publishing company

Cover image © Shutterstock, Inc.

**Kendall Hunt**
publishing company

www.kendallhunt.com
*Send all inquiries to:*
4050 Westmark Drive
Dubuque, IA 52004-1840

Copyright © 2011 by Dr. Denise C. Lagos

ISBN 978-1-4652-5349-1

Printed in the United States of America

# DEDICATION

*This book is dedicated to the loving memory of my beautiful parents, Louis and Penelope Katsafados, and to my maternal grandmother Chrisoula Sampatakos for emphasizing in such a special way the importance of an education and for instilling in me the love for learning.*

# CONTENTS

# ACKNOWLEDGMENTS

Recognition is extended to my many students who have been and continue to be committed and dedicated to the successful completion of *The Career Research Project*. The interview component of this project has afforded the students apprenticeships as well as job offerings in their field of study. The students have recognized the importance of the project with its experiential learning component and have appreciated the positive outcomes.

I especially express my deepest gratitude to my former students Rommel Magallanes, Daniel Zielinski, and Andrea Oviedo Amador, and their respective informants, Nurse Neri Jocelyn Gavina-Lorenzana, Automotive Specialist Tomas Berila, and Hotel Manager Michael Marino who generously shared their exemplary career ethnographic interviews. The outstanding interviews and research papers serve as models for other learners.

Many thanks go to Lasahin Griffin and Laura Leitner for all their help typing this manuscript. I appreciate their patience and constant support.

Additionally, I wish to wholeheartedly thank my family, my husband Harry, and my children Louis and Penelope for their continued encouragement, support and love throughout the years.

# ABOUT THE AUTHOR

Dr. Denise C. Lagos is a Senior Professor of English/English as a Second Language at Union County College. She has been teaching at UCC since 1980. Her degrees include a Bachelor of Arts from Fairleigh Dickinson University, Master of Arts in Teaching from Montclair State College, Master of Arts in Reading from Rutgers, Master of Arts in Administration and Supervision of Higher Education from Rutgers University, and a Master of Arts in English Literature from Drew University. Her Doctorate Degree in Language Education is from Rutgers University.

As a language educator, Dr. Lagos has helped thousands of students through Union County College as English as a Second Language Coordinator for the Cranford Campus. She is an advisor and editor to *The Foreign Student Voice*, UCC's literary publication, and is responsible for the design, layout, editing and distribution of the publication. She has given numerous lectures and workshops on language and culture, second language acquisition, and English and reading instruction theory and practice, including methodology and technique.

Dr. Lagos is the recipient of numerous awards, The Woman of Excellence Award in Education in Union County, The Marcom Publication Award, and UCC Presidential Commendations. She additionally serves as a mentor/supervisor to teachers in the public and private sectors from K-12 in New Jersey. She speaks three languages and holds certifications in seven areas of study. She continues to serve on numerous college committees and on the board of statewide professional organizations, including serving as editor to several Middle States of New Jersey Periodic Review Reports.

Dr. Denise Lagos resides in Chatham, New Jersey where she lives with her husband and two children, Louis and Penelope. Her four-legged family members include a handsome American Pit Bull named Cassius and two beautiful felines, a tabby named Athena, and a tortoise shell named Peanut.

# Chapter ONE
## OVERVIEW

 **What Is Research?**

In the broadest sense of the word, the definition of research includes any gathering of data, information, and facts for the advancement of knowledge. Research must be systematic and follow a series of steps and a rigid standard protocol. Research must be organized and undergo planning, which requires some kind of interpretation and opinion from the researcher.

There are various approaches in research to gather information and data for the researcher. Quantitative and qualitative methods are the methods frequently utilized by the researchers. Many researchers prefer one approach over the other. Yet, many other researchers agree that these two research methods need each other more often than not. However, because typically qualitative data involve words and quantitative data involve numbers, there are some researchers who feel that one is better—more scientific—than the other.

 **The Approach: Qualitative versus Quantitative Inquiry**

Over the years, there has been a great deal of complex discussion and debate surrounding the topic of research methodology and the theory of how inquiry should proceed. Much of the debate has centered on the issue of qualitative versus quantitative approaches to inquiry. Different methodologies become popular at various social, political, historical, and cultural times in our development. All methodological approaches have their specific strengths and weaknesses. These differences should be acknowledged and addressed by the researcher. Certainly, when you begin to think about your research methodology, you need to think about the differences between qualitative and quantitative approaches to research.

### Qualitative Research

The qualitative research approach explores attitudes, behaviors, and experiences through such methods as interview and participant observation. It attempts to get an in-depth opinion from the participant. Attitudes, behaviors, and experiences are important. The techniques employed in qualitative research are the ethnographic interview and participant observation.

### Quantitative Research

The quantitative research approach generates statistics through the use of large-scale survey research, with the utilization of such techniques as questionnaires and structured interviews.

Quantitative and qualitative research approaches have arisen from different research needs. The quantitative research approach endlessly pursues facts, whereas the qualitative research approach recognizes that the researcher's viewpoint is central. The quantitative research approach is used when the researcher desires to obtain entire trends or statistical truth in the research, whereas the qualitative research approach is used if the researcher wants to observe in detail his/her own research viewpoint.

**Qualitative versus Quantitative Research:**
**Features of Qualitative and Quantitative Research**

| Qualitative | Quantitative |
| --- | --- |
| The aim is a complete, detailed description. | The aim is to classify features, count them, and construct statistical models in an attempt to explain what is observed. |
| Researcher may only know roughly in advance what he/she is looking for. | Researcher knows clearly in advance what he/she is looking for. |
| Recommended during earlier phases of research projects. | Recommended during latter phases of research projects. |
| The design emerges as the study unfolds. | All aspects of the study are carefully designed before data are collected. |
| Researcher is the data gathering instrument. | Researcher uses tools such as questionnaires or equipment to collect numerical data. |
| Data are in the form of words, pictures, or objects. | Data are in the form of numbers and statistics. |
| Subjective—individual interpretation of events is important, e.g., utilization of participant observation, in-depth interviews. | Objective—seeks precise measurement and analysis of target concepts, e.g., utilization of surveys, questionnaires. |
| Qualitative data are more "rich," time consuming, and less able to be generalized. | Quantitative data are more efficient, able to test hypotheses, but may miss contextual detail. |
| Researcher tends to become subjectively immersed in the subject matter. | Researcher tends to remain objectively separated from the subject matter. |

 **Ethnographic Research: Ethnography**

Ethnography means trying to understand behavior and culture by going out and talking to people wherever they are, while they are doing whatever it is they do. It means entering someone's world for a while, be it a couple of hours or a couple of days, or like an anthropologist, for an extended period of time, perhaps a year.

A major difference between ethnography and other types of research is the depth and intimacy of the work. In ethnographic research, the researcher gets up close and personal to the research participants. The ethnographer spends time with people in a natural context of their daily lives. The researcher watches the world with a wide-angle lens, watching, listening, and learning. All of this is done in the context of where the action normally occurs: in the home, at the work place, or wherever.

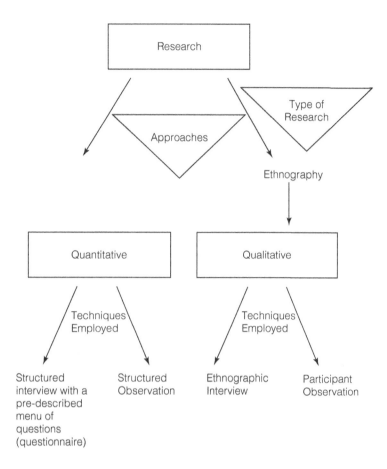

In ethnographic, qualitative research, the ethnographer goes into the study with very few preconceived notions and no script. The words and actions of the participant are key findings. Anthropologists, sociologists, and several linguists engage in this type of research. Qualitative research is inductive and a hypothesis is not needed to begin research. The researcher can learn the most about a situation by participating and/or being immersed in it.

 ## Choosing a Major/Career

The topic of the career research project is the individual student's career choice. Often times, students in their first several years of college have a difficult time deciding which career path they will follow. Choosing a career is a big decision. After all, the average person spends about 40 or more hours a week at work, and it is no wonder we want to be content with our work and enjoy what we are doing.

Choosing a major for pursuit of a career path is a very difficult decision for students beginning their college academic journey. Students sometimes flounder and are not quite sure about the major they should pursue in college or their career path. Choosing a major, thinking about a career, and getting an education—these are the things that college is all about. Yes, there are some students who arrive on campus and know exactly their major and career ambitions, but the majority of students do not. There is no need to rush into a decision about your major as soon as you arrive on campus. A majority of students in all colleges and universities change their major at least once in their college careers, and many change their major several times over the course of their college education.

As students begin their journey toward discovering that ideal career path, they must spend time brainstorming about it before making a decision. Students should not be discouraged if they do not have a major the first time they take this journey. The goal for the students should be narrowing their focus from all possible majors to a few areas that they can explore in greater depth.

Many colleges and universities offer their students a double major, some triple majors, and most schools have minors as well as majors. Your major in college is important for your first job after graduation, but studies have shown that most people will change careers. Many people change their careers approximately four or five times over the course of their lives, and there is no major that exists that can prepare a person for that!

There are several steps for students to consider before selecting a major.

*Step 1:* Students must examine and do a self-assessment of their individual interests. They should ask questions such as:

- What types of jobs or careers appeal to you?
- What types of things are interesting, fascinating, or exciting to you?

Going to your school's counseling center, going on-line, and taking appropriate tests will help you narrow down your areas of interest. Brainstorm with family and friends, discussing possible career choices. Exchanging opinions and ideas with those you trust may be very helpful in your decision-making process.

*Step 2:* Students must take into consideration their abilities. An examination of one's abilities and recognizing one's strengths and weaknesses are extremely important. What kind of skills do you have? Self-examination should begin by having the student look at courses taken in high school. What were the students' best subjects? Is there a pattern of interest? What kinds of extracurricular activities did you participate in while in high school? What kinds of things did you learn from part-time or summer jobs?

*Step 3:* Students should examine what they value in work. What do you value in your job, your career, and your work? Examples of values include: helping society, working under pressure, group affiliation, stability, security, status, pacing, working alone or with groups, having a positive impact on others, and many more.

Again, visiting a school's counseling center and going on-line to various career sites will help.

*Step 4:* Students must consider doing a career exploration. Students must ask: What career choices do I have with a major in...? Going on Web sites and learning about various occupations are important.

*Step 5:* Students must do a reality check. The need to honestly evaluate your options is an important final step. As a student, you may have an interest in a particular field, and see the value of the work, but may not have the skills required to do the job. Does your occupation require an advanced degree, but your future commitments preclude graduate study? Do you have an interest in the arts, but your family is convinced you should own a business like your father?

During a reality check, the students will become aware of obstacles, face them, and be realistic about whether they can get around them.

*Step 6:* Students have the task of narrowing down their choices and focusing on choosing a major. The career research project class requirement will force the student to decide upon a major and possible career choice. Based on all the students' research and self-assessment, they will have a better idea of the careers/majors they are not interested in pursuing as well as a handful of potential careers/majors that do interest them.

Students must be mindful of all the resources they have available, which will enable them to gather more valuable information about their major and career, bringing them one step closer to making a decision. Students should take advantage of:

- ***College's course catalog***—There is a wealth of information a student can find—from required courses to specialized majors.

- *Professors,* including advisers/counselors—It behooves students to talk to their professors, whether the student has taken a class with the professor or not—many professors have worked in the field which they teach and all are experts about careers and career opportunities.
- *Classmates,* especially upperclassmen—These students are further along in their studies, perhaps even involved in an internship or gone through job interviews.... This group of students will serve as a resource to gather more information.
- *College's alumni*—Your college has active alumni, many of whom like to talk with current students. They will serve as a resource to further gain valuable information.
- *Family and friends*—A wealth of information is right in front of you...talk to the people you trust the most who have your best interest at heart—they for sure will embrace you with guidance, experience, and additional information.
- *College's counseling center*—Counselors and advisers have a wealth of information at their fingertips—students must take advantage of these professionals' help. Be a familiar face to these experts, for they have resources for choosing a major and a career.

Once the student has decided upon a possible major/career choice, then they will be ready to begin their career research project.

 ## The Career Research Project

The career research project consists of three major components:

1. The ethnographic qualitative interview
2. The research paper
3. The oral presentation

The three chapters that address each component are:

Chapter 2: The Ethnographic Qualitative Interview

Chapter 3: The Research Paper

Chapter 4: The Oral Presentation

### *Career Research Project Objectives*

Students will be able to:

- Focus on career decision making.
- Conduct an ethnographic qualitative interview.
- Demonstrate competency in the process of writing a research paper using APA style.
- Demonstrate an ability to independently revise and edit their writing.
- Effectively paraphrase and avoid plagiarizing.
- Independently incorporate primary and secondary sources to support and refute ideas.
- Hone public speaking skills, including using a clear voice and timing a speech.
- Hone multimedia skills in the preparation of visual and auditory aids for an oral presentation.
- Acquire teaching skills in the preparation of material to demonstrate to an audience in an oral presentation.

# Chapter TWO
# THE ETHNOGRAPHIC INTERVIEW: PARTICIPANT OBSERVATION

 **General Ethnographic Interview**

Ethnographic interviewing is a type of qualitative research that combines immersive observation and directed one-on-one interviews. In anthropology, ethnographic researchers spend years living immersed in the cultures they study in order to understand behaviors and social rituals of an entire culture. Ethnographic interviewers apply this technique to understand the behaviors of people interacting with one another in a particular environment.

The ethnographic interview is a particular speech event. Every culture has many social occasions identified by the kind of talking that takes place in our society. Whether the talking is a lecture, a job interview, or a friendly conversation, the particular speech event is easily recognized. All speech events have cultural rules for beginning, ending, taking turns, asking questions, pausing, and the environment in which the conversation takes places.

The ethnographic interview is a qualitative technique that studies the cultural patterns of participants in their natural setting. The ethnographic interview is a friendly conversation, informal, unstructured, and a free elicitation of verbal exchange. The interviewer has no predescribed menu of questions in hand. When examining the ethnographic interview as a speech event, it must be stressed that the conversation is friendly and informal. The ethnographic general elements of this type of interview include:

1. Greetings: When people meet, they never begin talking without some form of greeting, usually verbal and nonverbal.
2. Asking questions: General questions will be asked on the onset of the interview as well as the conclusion, with more specific questions asked in the body of the interview.
3. Expressing cultural interest and expressing cultural ignorance: These two elements must be expressed by the interviewer to promote and perpetuate more conversation. The questions themselves indicate interest in the respondent. The body of the interviewer is the appropriate time for the ethnographer to emphasize and express these elements. Examples of statements that express cultural interest and ignorance are: "Oh really. I did not know that. It sounds interesting. Please tell me more."

4. Taking turns: An implicit cultural rule for friendly conversations, turn taking helps keep the encounter balanced. We all have experienced violations of this rule and know how it may lead to a sense of uneasiness or even anger. Do not interrupt when your informant is speaking.

5. Pausing: If the ethnographer and the respondent have been talking a while, and the interviewer is at a loss of what to ask next, a brief silence emerges when neither person feels it necessary to speak. Pausing indicates closure. The interviewer must ask, "Is there anything else I need to know that I have not yet asked you?" This may or may not perpetuate more conversation, depending upon the response of the informant.

6. Leave taking: Friendly conversations never stop without some verbal ritual that indicates closure.

 ## The Career Ethnographic Interview

A major component of the career research project is the ethnographic interview.

### *The Purpose of the Interview*

The purpose of the interview is for the student to find out all they can about their respective career choice. Has the student made the right decision about their career path? Often times, students are indecisive about their career choice.

### Criteria for Selection of Your Professional

Who shall the student select to interview?

- The informant must be a professional whom the student has never met. Networking can be advantageous to the student.
- The informant must be practicing the student's specific career choice, for example, if a student wants to become a college English professor, then he or she should not interview a high school English teacher.
- The informant must be educated in the United States of America. It is beneficial to the student to learn about the educational requirements of his or her career choice.
- The informant must be practicing in the profession for approximately 5 years or more. Students must avoid selecting an informant who has recently graduated from college and has no hands-on experience. And, on the contrary, they must not select an informant who is ready to retire or has already retired. The student may not receive updated methodological and technological data regarding the field.

### *How Will I Find the Professional?*

This is, in and of itself, a process. Selecting an outstanding, highly regarded professional is the key. Students can seek advice, direction, and guidance from their own professors in the field. Their very own peers in class may know the perfect professional to recommend. They can go to the work environment and do some sleuthing to find the right informant. Going online and finding professional Web sites in the field may also be another avenue to pursue. People who the students interact with on a daily basis may connect them to a professional in the field.

Each student should have three informant choices that they prioritize. The student's first choice of a possible informant may decline their request for an interview. Therefore, a second and third choice of a professional is a must. A back up plan is necessary, especially as there are time constraints and deadlines to meet during a busy, hectic semester.

### *How Do I Set Up the Appointment With the Professional?*

The students will first reach out to their first choice of an informant. Means of communication is by telephone or in person, *not* by email. If a professional does not recognize an email address, they may delete the email before even opening it. The most efficient, expedient way to connect is by telephone or in person.

If the students decide to set up the appointment with the professional in person, then they must have a recording device in hand in the event the professional agrees to the interview at the time of the request.

### *What Do I Say?*

a. Identify yourself
   "Hello" (address the professional with his or her proper title, no first names!)
   "My name is _____."
   "You don't know me, but you have been highly recommended by _____."
   Or
   "You don't know me, however, I have viewed your Web site and am extremely impressed with your expertize and accomplishments in the field."
   **Stroke your informant.** Stroking is a technique used in the ethnographic interview. To stroke is to compliment your informant.

b. Purpose: Brief description of the project
   The students must state the explicit purpose of the call or why they have approached the potential informant.
   "I am calling or I have come to ask you to help me."
   "I am a student at *name of your college or university*, and I am taking an English class. My professor has assigned a career research project. One of the major components of this project is to conduct an ethnographic interview with a professional in my career choice. I would like to be *name of profession* like you are."                                                    (Example: A registered nurse)

c. Interview Must be recorded (stress confidentiality)
   "One of the requirements of this interview is that it must be recorded, however, I can assure you that our conversation will be kept confidential and will only be heard by my professor for the purpose of evaluating my performance as an interviewer."

If your first choice of an informant declines your request for an interview, do not make any attempt to change the professional's mind. An unwilling participant, who does not have time to devote to the interview, will not give you the information that you are looking for about the career, thus the interview process will be an unsuccessful one. Thank the potential informant, and ask if he or she knows anyone in the profession who would be willing to participate in such an interview.

Because time is of the essence, the students must move quickly, not get discouraged, and go to their second and perhaps third choice of an informant. Your back up plan is a must in this process. Patience, determination, and perseverance are essential attributes that the student must possess during this process.

Length of Interview: 10 or more minutes minimum requirement

The students must remember that the objective/goal of the ethnographic interview is to find out everything that they personally want to learn about their career choice. They are like a sponge soaking up valuable, easy access information regarding their career pursuit.

### *What Recording Device Should I Use?*

Any type of recording device is acceptable. It is the student's responsibility to be certain that the recording device is operable. The recording of the interview must be audible and clear. The interviewer will include the information from the interview in the text of their career research paper. Additionally, the professor needs to listen to the interview in order to evaluate the student as the interviewer.

The student must include the following information on the recording, either before or after the interview.

- Record date, time, and place of the interview
- Record interviewer's name (student's name)
- Record interviewee's name (professional's name)
- Record a brief description of the career and the professional's job description

 **NOTE:**
The interview must be conducted in the professional's workplace.
Be on time or even early to your interview.
Dress professionally—as you would for a job interview.
The student sets the mood/tone of the interview environment.

Relax, be calm, and collected. Nervous behavior is contagious and will make your interviewee uncomfortable.

### *Content of the Career Ethnographic Interview*

Each student interview will have an evident introduction, body, and conclusion. The introduction and conclusion are very much alike.

**Introduction**

Each student will emphasize how thankful, grateful, and appreciative he or she is to the professional. The technique of stroking (to compliment) is also included in the beginning of the interview. The student will say—"Thank you so very much *professional's name* for allowing me to interview you. You are so highly regarded in your field. I know I will learn a great deal from you today, not only for this career research project, but for my future. I appreciate the sharing of your valuable time and your expertise."

The students must express these words of thanks in a meaningful sounding, animated way.

The students will begin with a general open-ended question that they have in mind before going to the interview. Examples of initial questions are: Describe a typical day at your job? How did you become interested in this career? How did you become the professional you are today?

**Body**

The content of the body of the interview will vary from student to student. After the students ask the first general question, depending upon the response of the informant, the interview content will proceed in a variety of directions. It is important for the students to remember that they will *not* have a menu of questions before them. The questions the interviewer poses will be based on the respondent's answers to the interviewer's previous question. General as well as more technical, specific related questions regarding the career will be asked by the interviewer. The ethnographic interview is informal, unstructured, and a free elicitation of verbal exchange. The interviewer's questions to the informant will be based not only on the informant's responses but also based on the ethnographer's research data that they will be compiling for their research paper. The students will be perusing the literature for the career paper prior to conducting the interview with the professional. Therefore, the students will be able to ask more methodological as well as technological specific related questions about the career.

### Types of Questions to Ask

1. Descriptive Questions: This type of question enables the interviewer to collect an ongoing sample of an informant's language. Descriptive questions are the easiest to ask and they are used in all interviews, for example, "Describe a typical day at your job?" "Could you tell me what you do at the office?" and "Could you describe the conference you attended?"

2. Structural Questions: This type of question enables the ethnographer to discover information about domains, the basic units in an informant's cultural knowledge, for example, "What are the educational requirements for this career?" "How does one get promoted in this field?" and "What are all the stages in getting transferred in your company?"
   Structural questions require an "x, y, z" response and are often repeated, so that if an informant identified six types of activities, the ethnographer might ask, "Can you think of any other kind of activities you would do as a hair stylist?"

3. Contrast Questions: This type of question enables the ethnographer to discover what an informant means by the various terms he or she used during the interview. Contrast questions enable the ethnographer to reveal the dimensions of meaning which informants employ to distinguish the objects and events in a particular environment. A typical contrast question is,

   "What is the difference between data entry and data analysis?"

   "What is the difference between giving an injection to a patient and drawing blood from a patient?"

The students must keep in mind to avoid posing questions that require a "Yes or No" response. Descriptive, structural, and contrast questions require a lengthy informant response that enables the ethnographer to ask more questions based on the informant's lengthy response.

The students must also remember that the technique of expression of cultural ignorance (explained earlier in this chapter) has to be utilized in the body of the ethnographic interview, for example, "Oh, really, I did not know this. How interesting. Please tell me more."

This technique of cultural interest and ignorance perpetuates more conversation, which ultimately furnishes the interviewer with more valuable information about their career choice.

4. Clarification Questions: This type of question gives the interviewer an opportunity to clarify informant responses that were not understood by the researcher, for example, "What do you mean when you say _____?"

### Conclusion

How does a student know when it is time to conclude the interview? Remember the objective/goal of the ethnographic interview is to perpetuate conversation. Realistically, the interview cannot go on for hours, as the informant has duties and responsibilities to resume in the work environment. As the interview progresses and time has elapsed, there will be inevitably pausing that will occur. Pausing is a lull of silence; the interviewer and the informant are not speaking. This indicates to the interviewer closure of the interview. At this time, the ethnographer will pose the concluding question:

"Is there anything else I need to know about this career that I have forgotten to ask you?"

At this point, depending on the informant's response to the above question, this will determine if the interview will continue or not. If there is in fact something additional about the career that the informant feels that the interviewer should know further information about, then the interview will continue, whereby the interviewer must pose the above question again after the additional information is conversed about. However, if the respondent feels the interviewer has asked all the necessary questions, then the interviewer will end the interview.

As stated earlier in the introduction section of the interview content, the content of both introduction and conclusion are very much alike. Each student at this point will reiterate to the professional how thankful, appreciative, and grateful they are to have been given this golden opportunity of having an interview with such a highly regarded professional. The technique of stroking must continue at the closure of the interview. The student must say,

"Thank you so much for the sharing of your valuable expertise and time. The information that you have furnished me about the career has been not only helpful to me for this career research project, but this interview, most importantly, has helped me for the future. I can clearly understand why you are a highly regarded professional in the career. Again, thank you so very much."

**Interruptions**

Because the interview will be conducted in the informant's workplace, interruptions are inevitable. If the interviewer needs to stop the recorder at any time during the interview process because of an interruption, such as a knock on the door, a telephone call, or other work-related interruptions, then it is the responsibility of the interviewer to remember where they left off. When the informant is ready to resume the interview, the conversation will continue with ease. Therefore, the interruption will not impact the interview in a negative way. The interviewer must stay calm and collected and utilize the interruption as a time to become the participant observer.

 **NOTE: Several sample student interviews are included on a CD for the student to listen to.**

**Confidentiality/Ethics**

Students must adhere to the following ethical points:

1. Honor your informant's privacy.
2. There is a difference in informant's time commitment to you when you do participant observation in a public place and when they do an interview with you. Always let your participants know what is expected of them and what they can expect of you and the process.
3. Unless otherwise agreed to, the informant's identity should be protected so that the information that you collect does not embarrass or in other ways harm them.

4. Treat informants with respect and seek cooperation with them throughout the research process.
5. In negotiating permission to conduct your interview, you must stress confidentiality and privacy to your informant regarding interview recorded content.
6. Tell the truth when you write up your interview and research findings.

 **Ethnographic Interview**

### *The Student Checklist*

What is an ethnographic interview?

- An informal, unstructured interview
- A friendly conversation
- A free elicitation of verbal exchange
- Your questions are developed based on your informant's responses.

### *Criteria for Informant Selection*

a. Must be a professional you have never met
b. Must be practicing your specific career choice
c. Must be educated in the United States of America
d. Must be in the profession for approximately 4 to 5 or more years

### *Set up Appointment to Conduct Interview*

- By telephone
- In person
- Length of interview: 10 or more minutes minimum requirement
  - Identify yourself
  - Purpose of the call
  - Brief description of project
  - Tape (stress confidentiality)
    - Record interviewer's name (your name)
    - Interviewee's name (professional)
    - Describe career
    - Place, date, and time of interview

A major letter grade will be given for the ethnographic interview.

### *Participant Observation*

Anthropologists have investigated over time the relationship between what people say and what they do or the relative importance of talking to informants as opposed to watching them. Imagine a world where only two positions are possible. If you take the first position, you would argue that the only way to learn about people would be to talk with them in private in an isolated room. If you take the other position, you would not listen to anything people say about what they do, but just observe their movements, both being ridiculous choices.

Most anthropologists would agree that sometimes people do what they say and other times they do not, arriving at the conclusion that both kinds of data, interview and participant observation, are needed in research. Intuitively, we know that there are important differences in the sources from which an ethnographer learns. If you watch people doing things, you learn something you cannot get by just talking with them, although you cannot learn much unless you do talk with them, before, during, and after the event.

Observation and interview mutually interact with each other, either simultaneously or sequentially, in the course of doing ethnography. Perhaps this frequent mutual interaction is one reason why they are so difficult to separate. Observation is critical in enriching our ability to give accounts of events. Informants, giving accounts in interviews, may leave things out. They may do so for any number of reasons. Informants, like ethnographers, have their "personal equation" that influences how they see things and what they report. In the ethnographer/informant relationship, the informant may judge that certain parts of an event account should be left out as while others should be emphasized. Several details of the account may be left out as "unimportant" or "obvious" when, in fact, they represent important information for the ethnographer to learn. The informant may simply forget some details or perhaps be misinformed, or, on the basis of limited experiences, give an idiosyncratic account.

In the career research project, the student is not only the interviewer, but the participant observer as well. Both techniques of the qualitative approach go hand in hand. Arriving to the interview appointment early will give the ethnographer a chance to observe what is going on in the work environment. While the interview is being conducted in the work place, further observation can occur. At the conclusion of the interview, the informant may invite the researcher to go on a tour of the work place, or the interviewer may request such a tour. For example, if the student is interviewing a teacher, then the student should request an observation of the class, either before or after the interview has been conducted. If feasible, the recording device should be kept on during the observation. As a participant observer, the student can validate the informant responses from the interview. For example, if an informant states that the work environment is exceptionally busy, then the observer can validate this statement based on what they observe in the workplace.

Additionally, an informant may be inconsistent in the account given, hence resulting in contradictions between an informant's account, the ethnographer's observation, and the literature data. Consequently, all the accounts are necessary to substantiate the findings.

## A Mock Career Ethnographic Interview

| Ethnographic Interview | Analysis |
|---|---|
| Ethnographer: Hi Penny. How are you? Thank you so very much for consenting to do this interview with me. You have been highly recommended by the owner of this beautiful restaurant as well as by many of your coworkers. You are going to help me not only with my career research project, but, more importantly, with my future. | Greetings |
| | Expression of thanks and appreciation |
| | Stroking |
| Informant: It is my pleasure, and I am pleased to talk to you today. | |

**A Mock Career Ethnographic Interview (Continued)**

| Ethnographic Interview | Analysis |
| --- | --- |
| Ethnographer: As I told you on the phone, I'm interested in understanding your work as a server in an upscale restaurant. I know you have had a lot of experience. Can you describe a typical day at your job? | Descriptive open-ended question (good initial question) |
| Informant: Well, first I should say that there's no typical day at the restaurant. | |
| Ethnographer: Well, that's fine, just go through any day and tell me what you think might usually happen. | Ethnographer's questions are based on the previous response of the informant |
| Informant: It depends if I have the lunch shift or the dinner shift. | |
| Ethnographer: What is the difference between the two shifts? | Contrast question |
| Informant: Well, for starters, the lunch shift is much more chaotic and stressful than the dinner shift. | |
| Ethnographer: Oh, really, now as a customer, I thought the dinner shift would be more stressful. I am surprised to hear you say that. I didn't know that. Why is this? | Expression of cultural interest and cultural ignorance |
| Informant: The luncheon crowd, a group of business people, have about an hour for lunch, so there are a lot of time constraints. Customers are not having a leisurely dinner, but a rushed lunch. | |
| Ethnographer: How are the gratuities in both shifts? Is there a big difference in the dollar amount? | Contrast questions |
| Informant: Actually, there are many times I make more money during the lunch shift. It is usually very busy and we have a huge turnover. | |
| Ethnographer: Really, I would have thought you made more money at dinner. I had no idea. Do you ever make more money during the dinner hour? | Expression of cultural interest and cultural ignorance |
| Informant: Sometimes, it depends if I have large parties. If I have several parties of 6–8 people, then yes, I do make a lot more. | |

*continued*

**A Mock Career Ethnographic Interview (Continued)**

| Ethnographic Interview | Analysis |
|---|---|
| Ethnographer: When you have a large party, is the gratuity added automatically to the total amount of the bill? | |
| Informant: Yes, 15% is added to the total and often the customer will give me an additional gratuity. I do, however, have to split my gratuities with the bus boys as well as the bartender. | |
| Ethnographer: Really! How much do you have to give your coworkers? How does the restaurant decide this? What is the procedure? | Expression of cultural interest<br><br>Structural questions |
| Informant: At the end of the shift, it is the policy of the restaurant that each server counts their gratuities. The bus boys get 10% of total amount of your gratuities, and the bartender gets 5%. It all works out well. | |
| Ethnographer: So would you say that this job overall is lucrative? | |
| Informant: Yes, I make a decent living, and I can comfortably pay my bills. | |
| Ethnographer: What are your daily duties and responsibilities of this job every day? | Structural question |
| Informant: Well, if I am working the lunch shift, I go in at 10 in the morning. The restaurant opens at noon. The servers get in 2 hours earlier for set up. Each week, each server has assigned duties. For example, this week I have been assigned to several tasks like making sure the tables are clean, having the proper utensils on the table, filling up all the condiments, and setting up the bar. | |
| Ethnographer: When you say filling up all the condiments, what exactly are you referring to? | Clarification question |
| Informant: I mean filling up the salt and pepper shakers, the mustard, and ketchup bottles. | |
| Ethnographer: I am surprised to hear you have to set up the bar. I thought only the bartender or barmaid did that. | Expression of cultural ignorance |
| Informant: They help us, but ultimately it is the server's responsibility. | |

**A Mock Career Ethnographic Interview (Continued)**

| Ethnographic Interview | Analysis |
| --- | --- |
| Ethnographer: Yet, you give them 5% of your gratuities. I'm perplexed about this. It does not seem fair. | Restatement: The ethnographer repeats information of a previous response for clarification. |
| Informant: Yes, it is fine. The bartender or barmaid hustle to make the drinks for our tables, so customers aren't waiting for their drinks. They work very hard like we do, and they help the servers as much as they can. We all get along really well. It is a team effort. | |
| Ethnographer: Does the owner of this restaurant subscribe to any journals in the field, or do you have any pamphlets, brochures or menus you can share with me for my career research paper? | |
| Informant: Yes, we have plenty of restaurant food and beverage publications here in the restaurant. I subscribe to a culinary publication, since I am interested in going to a culinary school to become a chef in the future. I can give you a lot of literature. | |
| Ethnographer: Oh really! Culinary school sounds very interesting. I guess having the experience of being a server, will help you with your future plans, don't you think? | Expression of cultural interest and cultural ignorance |
| Informant: Oh yes, I know my experience will help me in culinary school. Even knowing the industry's terminology will be helpful for me. For example, if the chef or short order cook says, "Special number five on the menu is eighty-six," I know we are sold out of that item on the menu. | |
| Ethnographer: That's interesting. I didn't realize there are special terms used in a restaurant. I guess there are a lot of things I don't know about this business! | Expression of cultural interest and cultural ignorance |
| | Pausing |
| Ethnographer: Is there anything else that I need to know about this career that I have forgotten to ask? Is there anything else I should know? | Concluding questions |

*continued*

**A Mock Career Ethnographic Interview (Continued)**

| Ethnographic Interview | Analysis |
|---|---|
| Informant: You have done a great job covering everything! Would you like me to show you around the restaurant? There is a catering hall we have upstairs. We will go there first, and then I will take you to the kitchen. The publications I will give you for your paper are in the office, that will be our last stop. | |
| Ethnographer: Oh, this is terrific! I cannot thank you enough for all you have done for me today. The sharing of your time and expertise has been so valuable for me. I can certainly see why your coworkers and the owner of this restaurant recommended you as the perfect person to interview. This interview has helped me for my research project, but, most importantly, the information you have shared with me will help me for my future. Thank you again, very much! | Concluding remarks: expression of thanks and appreciation<br><br><br>Stroking |

# *Chapter* THREE
# THE RESEARCH PAPER

 **Getting Started: Gathering Data**

The student must begin to peruse the literature in their field of study. Perusal of the literature is not only essential in the preparation of the career research paper, but it is equally as important in the preparation of the ethnographic interview.

1. Go to the library—Go first to your own college library, then venture out to other college and university libraries. Your own town library is another option. Your first stop in any library should be at the reference desk. Do not feel intimidated to ask questions to the reference librarians. They will guide, direct, and respond to all your questions. Remember to utilize a variety of sources in your career research paper. A minimum requirement of six or more references must be used in your paper.

Types of references:

- Books
- Career Handbook or Career Encyclopedia

Located in the Periodical section of the Library

- Journals
- Magazines
- Newspapers
- Brochures
- Pamphlets
- Newsletters

*Journal* is a blanket term for a scholarly publication that is published periodically, generally either monthly or quarterly. A journal is distinct from a magazine in that journals are generally for a very specific audience: experts within a specific scholarly or professional field. Magazines, on the other hand, usually have a more general readership. While magazines sometimes report new or ongoing research, the information is often given second-hand. If an article in a magazine reports any kind of scholarly research, chances are that the information was originally presented in a journal.

The information contained in a journal article is often more valuable than the information found in books because turnaround time for journals is usually quite short. While it takes months or years for a book to be published, an article could conceivably be written, submitted, accepted, and published in a journal all in a matter of weeks. Thus, as journal articles generally present fresh, cutting-edge information, their value and validity in the research process cannot be understated.

There must be a minimum of **one** or more journals on your reference page. It is important for students to become familiarized with specialized publications as journals in their respective fields of study. Many professionals subscribe to journals in their field to keep abreast of new methodology and technology in their area of expertise.

2. Career Web sources

Go online—there are many career Web sites to investigate. If you see interesting sources online that you may possibly use in your career research paper, you must treat the reference as the source that it is, and *not* an electronic source, if possible. Be certain to print out the entire article, from beginning to end, and do a makeshift pagination once the source is printed out. Page numbers are needed for in-text citations and the reference page. Do not forget to print out cover pages of each source as well. This information on the beginning pages of a source will be needed by the researcher to include on the reference page.

3. Ethnographic interview—workplace

An excellent means of gathering data for your research paper is during the ethnographic interview. Upon arrival to the workplace, look for brochures, pamphlets, and newsletters that may be possible sources of information. During the interview, ask your informant which journals he or she subscribes to. Are any journals available to you, the researcher? The informant can be a great library source.

## *Organization of Career Research Paper*

APA format is the official style of the American Psychological Association (APA) and is commonly used to cite sources in psychology, education, and the social sciences. Most students have already used MLA style, Modern Language Association and are familiar with its guidelines. It is essential for the student to recognize the importance of learning a variety of writing style manuals. During their academic journey, students will be required to write papers in many different writing styles. If students have never utilized APA format previously, they may find that it is quite different from several of the writing styles and guidelines they may have previously used. While it may take a bit of getting used to a new manual, learning how to write an APA paper is a useful skill that will serve students well throughout their academic years.

The organization of a paper that adheres to the APA guidelines is rather simple to follow. Although the type of organization that follows is not in the APA manual, the guidelines permit modifications/variations, which meet the specifications of your assigned career research paper.

## *Components of Career Research Paper*

1. **Title page:** The title of your career in all caps in bold black face should be placed in the center of the page.

    To the bottom right is your full name, followed by the month/year that the paper is due—single-space those two lines.

    To the bottom left is the Professor's name, class name, and the Career Research Paper—single-space those three lines.

2. **Table of Contents:** Although not addressed in the APA manual, a table of contents will help the reader understand the organization of the paper and indicate to the reader the content within the paper.

Each student's paper will include an introductory section, labeling it according to its text, and interview data section, highlighting the noteworthy points of the ethnographic interview, and a concluding section, labeled accordingly. Each ethnographer will determine the remaining subheadings. The number of subheadings and the text within will vary in each student's paper.

 **NOTE:** If a formal participant observation has been done, then it is recommended that the ethnographer write up what he or she has observed in a separate section of the paper entitled, Participant Observation.

3. **Body: text of paper**

The career research paper must be *five* or more full pages in length with each subheading having at least *one* full page or more of text in the body of the paper. The researcher must adhere to general mechanical guidelines. These guidelines may be a slight variation of APA format, however, are an accommodation of the specified career research project.

a. Margins: One inch on all sides (top, bottom, left, right).

b. Font size and type: 12-point Times New Roman font.

c. Line spacing: Double-space throughout the paper.

d. Spacing after punctuation: Space *once* after commas, colons, and semicolons within sentences. Insert *two* spaces after punctuation marks that end sentences.

e. Alignment: Flush left—the text lines up on the left margin. The right-hand side of the text does not line up with the right-hand margin (creating uneven right margins).

f. Paragraph indentation: Five spaces.

g. Pagination: The page number may appear either (a) on the bottom right or (b) bottom middle (select your preference of numbering your paper). The title and table of content pages are not paginated. The researcher will begin pagination in the body of the paper, including every page thereafter.

h. Subheadings within body: As stated earlier in the Table of Contents section, each ethnographer is required to include an Introduction, Participant Observation (only if a formal observation was done during the interview appointment), Interview Data, and Conclusion sections. The remaining sections to be included in the body of the career research paper are determined by the researcher. Students should include areas of their career choice that spark their interest and furnish them with current information about their field.

Subheadings must be flushed left with a number preceding them. The name of each subheading must be short, clear, and concise, but not wordy. The subheading names in the Table of Contents are identical to the subheading names in the text of the paper.

1. Introduction
   The introductory subheading name will be determined by its text. Students must ask themselves:

   What do I want to include in this beginning section of my paper?

   Do I want to label this section, Interest, and include why the researcher became interested in this field?

   Do I want to investigate the history of my career choice and name this section, History?

2. Participant Observation
   This subheading (if included) must be placed before the Interview Data section. Basically, this section will include a description of what the researcher observed before, during, and

after the interview with the professional in the work environment. If a formal observation was done, then the student must describe what was observed in the setting.

Examples:

- Observing a classroom setting in session
- A tour of a hospital
- A tour of a physical therapy facility
- A doctor with his or her patient
- A tour of a construction site
- A ride in a police vehicle with an officer
- A veterinarian operating on an animal
- A radiologist explaining images

Appendix/ices subheading (optional) is placed after the reference page. If there are no appendices, then the reference page is the last page of your paper.

3. Interview Data

This subheading is placed before the concluding section. The purpose of this section is for the researcher to highlight the noteworthy, significant points of the ethnographic interview. Were there contradictions in the data collected from the research, interview, and participant observation? Did information from a journal article contradict something said by the informant during the interview? Did the researcher observe something in the work environment that was different than what was spoken about during the ethnographic interview? The Interview Data section may include excerpts paraphrased from the interview in a Q and A (question and answer) regarding interesting points of information about the career, but should *not* be a complete transcription of the interview. The student may additionally include an evaluation of the interview process. Was it difficult to find a professional to interview? Were there many interruptions during the interview? Was it noisy in the workplace? Did the researcher find the interview informative?

4. Conclusion

The concluding subheading will be determined by its text as in the Introduction. Students must ask themselves:

How do I want to end my paper?

Do I want to include my plans for the future?

As a result of this career research project, I have confirmed my decision to pursue my career choice, or I have changed my mind about my career choice.

## *Reference Page*

Students must adhere to the following APA format on the reference page.

- Your references must *begin on a new page*. Title the subheading: References and center the title text at the top of the page.
- All source entries must be in *alphabetical order*.
- The first line of each reference must be flush with the left margin. Each subsequent line is indented 5–6 spaces.
- Each reference's subsequent lines are single-spaced; however, be certain to *double or triple space* between references.

- All sources cited must appear both in-text and on the reference page.
- Titles of books, journals, magazines, newspapers, pamphlets, brochures, and newsletters should appear in italics.
- Begin with author's last name and first initial, if the author is identified.
- Place date of publication in parentheses immediately after the author's last name.
- For titles of books, capitalize only the first word of the title, the first word after a colon, and proper nouns.
- The first word in the title of a document (such as an article) should be capitalized.
- Titles of journals and other periodicals should have all major words capitalized.
- All words in the title of a Web site should be capitalized.
- Do not place titles of articles in quotation marks.
- Use the abbreviations "p." or "pp." before page numbers of newspaper articles and works in anthologies; do not use them before page numbers of articles appearing in magazines and scholarly journals.
- Alphabetize your list by the last name of the author or editor; if there is no author or editor, alphabetize by the first word of the title other than a, an, or the.
- The ethnographic interview (an unpublished interview) will *not* be listed as a reference on the reference page.

### *Appendices*

In the career research paper, any visual data included by the researcher will be considered an Appendix/ices (a deviation of APA format). For the purposes of this paper, figures, graphs, charts, diagrams, maps, photographs, and any other drawings will be named Appendix/ices. Each appendix will be labeled with a capital letter (e.g., Appendix A, Appendix B, Appendix C). When an appendix is referred to in the text, the researcher will include after that text (See Appendix A). The visual data will be placed after the reference page in the paper and will appear as follows:

Appendix A

Salary Increments

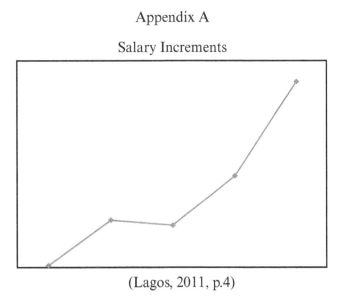

(Lagos, 2011, p.4)

---

 **NOTE:** An in-text parenthetical citation is needed below the visual data if it has been extracted from a source, and that source must be referenced on the reference page.

| Glossary of Terms | |
|---|---|
| Students must refer to themselves in the third person throughout the paper | |
| *Researcher*<br>*Ethnographer*<br>*Interviewer* | Students must *not* refer to themselves in the career research paper in the first person. No I, Me, My or Mine in the paper. |
| Students must refer to the person they interviewed as: | |
| *Professional*<br>*Informant*<br>*Respondent*<br>*Interviewee*<br><br>The career name:<br>e.g. the nurse<br>the police officer<br>the mechanic<br>the engineer | Students must *never* identify the professional they interviewed by their name. |
| He, She,<br>Him, Her | Acceptable pronouns |

## Research Paper

### The Student Checklist

a. Must be *typed* and *double-spaced*

b. APA format must be followed for (parenthetical citations) and references

c. Your research paper must consist of:

1. Title page
2. Table of Contents (must include an introduction, interview data, participant observation, and conclusion sections
3. Text of paper (five full pages—minimum)
4. (Parenthetical citations) within text of research paper (six minimum). At least *one* parenthetical citation per reference needed
5. References (sources used)—six minimum. Your sources may include: books, newspapers, magazines, journals, newsletters, pamphlets, brochures, career encyclopedia, and career handbook. One journal inclusion is a requirement.
6. Appendix(ices) (optional)

d. No "I," "Me," "My," or "Mine" in the paper. Refer to yourself as: the researcher, ethnographer, and interviewer. Refer to the person you interviewed as: the professional, interviewee, respondent, and informant. Pronouns (he or she, him or her) may be used as well.

e. No contractions—do not use can't, write out can not

f. No abbreviations initially—explain what an abbreviation means the first time it is presented: (FBI) Federal Bureau of Investigation

g. Do not use any content from Wikipedia or any related Web site run by the Wikimedia foundation

A major letter grade will be assigned for the research paper.

 **Overview**

*APA*

**In-text Parenthetical Citations and References**

In-text parenthetical citations give credit to sources used within the body of your paper. A writer must cite an author in the text when you (a) paraphrase from a source and (b) quote directly from a source, verbatim.

In-text citations additionally help direct the reader to the complete source included on your reference page. Do not list a source on the reference page unless you have parenthetically cited from the source at least one time in the paper. Six or more sources, one of which must be a journal, are required on the reference page. Remember all sources cited must appear both *in-text* and on the *reference page*. Any reference that appears in the text of your research paper must be included on the reference page, and any item appearing on your reference page must also be cited somewhere in the body of your text.

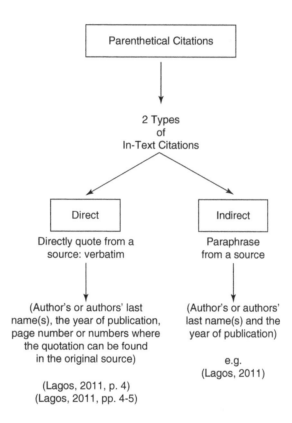

**Variations of In-Text Parenthetical Citations**

| **Direct** | **Indirect** |
|---|---|
| 1. Author named in your text e.g., Lagos (2011) states "_____" (p.3). | 1. Author named in your text e.g., Lagos (2011) indicates that _____. |
| 2. Author not named in your text e.g., "In 2009, registered nurses had a 5% increase in salary" (Lagos, 2011, p. 5). | 2. Author not named in your text e.g., A registered nurse's salary increased by 5% in 2009 (Lagos, 2011). |
| 3. Author and date cited in-text e.g., In a 2011 article, Lagos states "_____" (p. 4). | 3. Author and date cited in-text e.g., In a 2011 article, Lagos attributes that _____. |

## Direct In-Text Parenthetical Citations

### *Quantity Variations of Direct In-Text Citations*

Format differs depending upon the number of sentences the researcher is extracting from the source. Quotations containing (a) *three or less sentences* should be worked into the body of your paper. Longer quotations, (b) *four or more* sentences should be set apart from text as block quotations.

1. Shorter quotations (three or less sentences)
   - Keep in the body of text
   - Use double quotation marks to enclose text
   - Author's last name, year of publication, page number(s)

2. Longer quotations (four or more sentences)
   - Significantly indent on both the left and right sides of the quotation
   - Single space the text
   - Do *not* use double quotation marks to enclose text
   - Author's last name, year of publication, page number(s)

 **American Psychological Association (APA)**

 **NOTE:** No in-text parenthetical citations are needed in the Interview Data section of the career research paper unless information is pulled from a source other than the ethnographic interview. If, however, information from the interview is noted in another section of the paper, other than the Interview Data section, it must be parenthetically cited as (Communication), but not listed on the reference page. If the researcher acquires information through informal means such as a note, letter, email, telephone, radio, and television, then such data are considered as personal communication and are cited as (Communication) throughout the paper, but again, *not* listed as a source on the reference page.

# American Psychological Association (APA) Parenthetical Citations and References

**American Psychological Association Style**

The American Psychological Association (APA) requires citation of documentation within the text, rather than in footnotes or endnotes. The author's last name, the date of publication, and any other information necessary for locating the material cited may be incorporated into the text itself or placed within parentheses, as necessary for the particular sentence. An alphabetical reference list at the end of the research paper provides complete information about each source cited in the text. The specifications for creating the entries for numerous types of sources appear in the section entitled "Reference Forms." Instructions for organizing the list of references can be found in "The List of References."

**Parenthetical Reference Citations in Text**

Whether you paraphrase, summarize, or quote directly, you must provide the source of your information within the text. Documentation should be entered in a way that makes the identity of the source entirely clear while avoiding duplication and unnecessary clutter. As you write, you will want to keep in mind the need for parenthetical documentation, and occasionally you may want to revise a sentence to accommodate or reduce parenthetical material.

**Author named in your text**

If you mention the author's name in your text, cite only the date of publication in parentheses, immediately after the author's name.

Gould (1989) attributes Darwin's success to his gift for making the appropriate metaphor.

**Subsequent citation in same paragraph**

When another sentence in the same paragraph refers to the same author, the parenthetical material, if it remains the same, need not be repeated. In any subsequent paragraph, however, you would need to provide the parenthetical information again. Use the last name only in both first and subsequent citations, except when two authors have the same last name.

**Author not named in your text**

When you do not mention the author's name in your own text, that name, followed by a comma and the date of publication, appears in parentheses at the end of the sentence or, if you have referred to more than one source, at the end of the relevant clause.

As metaphors for the workings of nature, Darwin used the tangled bank, the tree of life, and the face of nature (Gould, 1989).

**Author and date cited in text**

If you use both the name of the author and the date in the text, a parenthetical reference is not needed.

In a 1989 article, Gould explores some of Darwin's most effective metaphors.

**Direct quotation with name of author**

When your sentence contains a quotation and includes the name of the author, place the publication date and page number in parentheses. Abbreviate the word *page* or *pages* (p. or pp.). The publication date follows the name of the author; the page number follows the end of the quotation.

> Gould (1989) explains that Darwin used the metaphor of the tree of life "to express the other form of interconnectedness–genealogical rather than ecological–and to illustrate both success and failure in the history of life" (p. 14).

**Direct quotation without name of author**

When you use a quotation but do not identify the author in the sentence, the name of the author, date of publication, and page number appear in parentheses at the end of the sentence, followed by the period for the sentence.

> Darwin used the metaphor of the tree of life "to express the other form of interconnectedness–genealogical rather than ecological" (Gould, 1989, p. 14).

**Work by two authors**

When you refer to a work by two authors, cite both names each time the reference appears. Use an ampersand (&) within the parentheses, but spell out the word *and* within your text.

> Sexual-selection theory has been used to explore patterns of insect mating (Alcock & Thornhill, 1983). Alcock and Thornhill (1983) also demonstrate....

**Three, four, five, or six authors**

For a work by more than two authors but fewer than seven, cite all names in the first reference. In subsequent references, cite only the name of the first author and use et al., for "and others."

> Scientists have isolated a gene connected to circadian rhythms in plants (Millar, Straume, Chory, Chua, & Kay, 1995, p. 1163).... They identified the mutations that activated light-dependent pathways (Millar et al., 1995, p. 1165)....

**Seven or more authors**

For a work by seven or more authors, give only the last name of the first author followed by et al. in both first and subsequent references.

> Scientists have constructed a deletion map of the human Y chromosome (Vollrath et al., 1992)....
> Their studies resolved a region of the chromosome into ordered intervals (Vollrath et al., 1992)....

**Distinguishing entries with multiple authors**

When two entries with multiple authors shorten to exactly the same form, cite as many names as you need to distinguish the two parenthetical references. If, in addition to the article in the previous example with Vollrath as first author followed by Foote, you had another in which the name Smith followed Vollrath, the two shortened references would appear this way:

> (Vollrath, Foote et al., 1992)... (Vollrath, Smith et al., 1992).

However, if these two articles were published in different years, the second name would not be necessary to distinguish them:

(Vollrath et al., 1992)... (Vollrath et al., 1993).

### Authors with the same last name

When you cite works by two or more authors with the same last name, use initials to identify the authors in the text, even if the dates of publication differ.

R. Dawkins (1986) and M. S. Dawkins (1980) contribute to an understanding of consciousness in animals.

### Work cited in another work

When the source of an indirect or direct quotation is a secondary source, refer to the source you actually used within parentheses and in the reference list.

Darwin's metaphors (as cited in Gould, 1989) ....

If you use a direct quotation from the secondary source, the parenthetical reference reads (as quoted by Gould, 1989, p. ?).

### Work identified by title

When a work is noted in the reference list by title alone, a shortened version of the title is used to identify the work parenthetically in the text. Within the text, whether in parentheses or not, titles are presented differently from the way they are in the reference list. All words are capitalized, except for articles, conjunctions, and prepositions of four letters or fewer; the title of a book, report, brochure, or periodical is italicized; and the title of an article or chapter appears within quotation marks.

The National Endowment for the Humanities supports "theoretical and critical studies of the arts" but not work in the creative or performing arts (*Guidelines*, 1994, p. 1). Changes in the Medical College Admissions Test to begin in 1991 are expected to encourage more students to pursue general studies in the humanities, natural sciences, and social sciences ("New Exam," 1989).

### Corporate author

When you cite a work by a group author, use the name of the corporation or organization as the author.

"Retired officers retain access to all of the university's educational and recreational facilities" (Columbia University, 1995, p. 54).

You may use well-known abbreviations of the name of a corporate author in subsequent parenthetical references or in the text itself. For example, you might use NSF for National Science Foundation, NIMH for National Institutes of Mental Health, and ERIC for Educational Resources Information Center.

In these cases, your first reference to the group or organization should include the abbreviation you intend to use.

*The Guidelines* (National Endowment for the Humanities [NEH], 1994) specify…The NEH gives block grants to states.…It funded a study of …(*Guidelines,* 1994).

### Work explicitly identified as anonymous

If the title page actually gives the author's name as "Anonymous," use that word for the author and omit the title: (Anonymous, 1925). You will find few such instances, particularly among recent works.

### Classical work

For a classical work, or any work so old that it was not published in the modern sense, cite the date of the translation you used: (Aristotle, trans. 1985). If the date of authorship is relevant, include it in your text. For identifying specific parts of a classical work, use conventional line, book, or section numbers, as appropriate for each particular case. The entry for the *Nicomachean Ethics* would read: (Aristotle, trans. 1985, 1123a34).

### Bible or other sacred writing

Refer to passages in the Bible with citations of book, chapter, and verse and place the translation you used within parentheses, but not in the reference list: Jeremiah 48.18 (New Revised Standard Version). APA uses a period rather than a colon between chapter and verse: 2 Cor. 15.2.

### Reference to more than one work

Parenthetical references may mention more than one work. Use commas between separate dates for works by the same author.

- List two or more works by the same author in order of date of publication: (Gould, 1987, 1989).
- Differentiate works by the same author with the same publication date by adding an identifying letter to each date: (Bloom, 1987a, 1987b). The letters also appear in the reference list, where multiple works from the same year are alphabetized by title.
- List works by different authors in alphabetical order by last name and use semicolons to separate the references: (Alcock & Thornhill; Gould, 1989).

The following list on the next page provides reference-list entries for the works used in these illustrations of APA reference citations.

# References

Alcock, J., & Thornhill, R. (1983). *The evolution of insect mating systems.* Cambridge, MA: Harvard University Press.

Anonymous. (1925). *The wind.* NY: Harper.

Aristotle. (1985). *Nicomachean ethics* (T. Irwin, Trans.). Indianapolis, IN: Hackett Publishing.

Bloom, H. (Ed.). (1987a). *Eugene O'Neill.* NY: Chelsea.

Bloom, H. (Ed.). (1987b). *John Dryden.* NY: Chelsea.

Columbia University. (1995). *Faculty handbook.* NY: Author.

Dawkins, M. S. (1980). *Animal suffering: The science of animal welfare.* London: Chapman.

Dawkins, R. (1986). *The blind watchmaker.* NY: Norton.

Gould, S. J. (1987). *Time's arrow, time's cycle: Myth and metaphor in the discovery of geological time.* Cambridge, MA: Harvard University Press.

Gould, S. J. (1989). The wheel of fortune and the wedge of progress. *Natural History, 89*(3), 14, 16, 18, 20–21.

*Guidelines.* (1994). Washington, DC: National Endowment for the Arts.

*Guidelines and application form for directors, 1996 summer seminars for school teachers.* (1994). Washington, DC: National Endowment for the Humanities.

*The Holy Bible.* (1989). (New Revised Standard Edition). Oxford, Eng.: Oxford University Press.

Millar, A. J., Straume, M., Chory, J., Chua, N.-H., & Kay, S. A. (1995, February 24). The regulation of circadian period by phototransduction pathways in Arabidopsis. *Science, 267,* 1163–1165.

New exam for doctor of future. (1989, March 15). *The New York Times,* p. B10.

Vollrath, D., Foote, S., Hilton, A., Brown, L. G., Beer-Romano, P., Bogan, J. S., et al. (1992, October 2). The human Y chromosome: A 43-interval map based on naturally occurring deletions. *Science, 258,* 52–60.

## *Reference Forms*

This section provides reference forms for a wide range of sources, from articles and books to electronic media. Because types of sources are proliferating rapidly, you may need to use some that are not mentioned here. In this case, you should look at the closest alternative and construct your own entry based on the basic principles of APA format. Also, you may have to refer to more than one of the examples given in this section. To create an entry for an article appearing in a book with three editors, for example, you would use the form for an article and the form for an edited book, following the rules for works with two or more authors.

## Periodicals

### Basic entry

The basic entry for an article in a periodical begins with the last name(s), followed by the initials (not the entire first names) of all authors. The year of publication follows in parentheses; for magazine and newspaper articles, give the month and day (if any) or the season (capitalized). Next, give the title of the article, not enclosed in quotation marks; the title of the periodical, including the article *the*, italicized through the end punctuation mark, if any; the volume number, also italicized along with the end punctuation mark, if any; and inclusive page numbers. A period follows the author, the date, the title of the article, and the end of the entry. The name of the periodical, the volume number, and the page numbers are separated by commas. Only the first word of the article title, the first word of the subtitle, and proper nouns and adjectives are capitalized. All words except articles and prepositions of fewer than four letters are capitalized in the title of the periodical, and the title is italicized. The abbreviation p. or pp. is used in references to daily newspapers but not to journals or magazines. Both numbers in inclusive pages include all digits.

### Article by one author

Simon, G. (1990). The significance of silence. *Paragraph, 13,* 202–216.

### Article by two authors

For an article by two authors, invert the names of both authors, using a comma to separate surnames and initials. Place an ampersand (&) before the name of the second author.

McLaren, P., & Estrada, K. (1993). A dialogue on multiculturalism and democratic culture. *Educational Researcher, 22,* 27–33.

### Article by three to six authors

List the names of all authors up to six, separating surnames and initials with a comma and placing an ampersand (&) before the name of the final author.

Dornbusch, S. M., Carlsmith, J. M., Bushwall, S. J., Ritter, P. L., Leiderman, H., & Hastorf, A. H. (1985). Single parents, extended households, and the control of adolescents. *Child Development, 56,* 326–341.

**Seven or more authors**

For an article with seven or more authors, list the first six names and use et al. (for "and others") to refer to the rest, no matter how many.

> Vollrath, D., Foote, S., Hilton, A., Brown, L. G., Beer-Romano, P., Bogan, J. S., et al. (1992, October 2). The human Y chromosome: A 43-interval map based on naturally occurring deletions. *Science, 258,* 52–60.

**Names with suffixes**

For names followed by a suffix such as Jr. or III, place the suffix after the initials for the first name, preceded and followed by a comma.

> Harper, C. L., Jr., Nyquist, L. E., Bansal, B., Wiesmann, H., & Shih, C.-Y. (1995, January 13). Rapid accretion and early difference of Mars. *Science, 267,* 213–216.

When the name appears in the text (in regular, rather than inverted, order), no punctuation separates the name and the suffix: C. L. Harper Jr., Charles S. Levings III.

**Journal paginated by issue**

If each issue of a journal begins with page 1, give the issue number in parentheses after the volume number without an intervening space. The issue number is not italicized.

> Brunsdale, M. M. (1991). Stages on her road: Sigrid Undset's spiritual journey. *Religion and Literature, 23(3),* 83–96.

**Magazine article**

The entry for an article in a magazine or newsletter with a volume number includes the month and day (if any), as well as the year, the volume, and the pages.

> Osborn, M. (1994, March 11). Status and prospects of women in science in Europe. *Science, 263,* 1389–1391.

Most magazines have volume numbers, although in popular publications they often are not featured prominently. If you ascertain that the magazine has no volume number, follow the format for a newspaper article. If no author is given, begin the entry with the title of the article.

**Newspaper article**

Entries for articles in newspapers are constructed according to the principles for magazines, except that the volume number is omitted and the abbreviation p. or pp. is used to indicate page(s).

> Morain, D. (1993, June 7). Poor counties hit hardest by budget cuts, *The Los Angeles Times,* p. A1.

**Newspaper article, unsigned**

An entry for a newspaper (or magazine) article without a byline or signature begins with the headline or title in the author position without italics or quotation marks.

> New exam for doctor of future. (1989, March 15). *The New York Times,* p. B10.

**Newspaper article, discontinuous pages**

When a newspaper article appears on discontinuous (nonconsecutive) pages, give all page numbers and separate the numbers with commas.

Broad, W. J. (1989, March 14). Flight of shuttle begins flawlessly. *The New York Times,* pp. Al, C7.

**Newspaper article in designated section**

When you cite a newspaper article with a special designation, indicate its nature in brackets following the title.

Williams, R. L. (1992, May 13). National university is an outmoded idea [Letter to the editor]. *The Chronicle of Higher Education,* p. B4.

**Special issue of a journal**

In an entry for a special issue of a journal, identify the editors (if any) of the issue and the title of the issue. If the issue does not specify its editors, the title of the issue occupies the author position.

Political and social issues in composition [Special issue]. (1992). *College Composition and Communication, 43(2), 6–7.*

**Monographs**

In an entry for a monograph, identify the nature of the material within brackets if the series or journal title does not, and give the volume number of the issue. Place additional identifying numerals, such as issue and serial (or whole) numbers, in parentheses after the volume number without an intervening space.

Hinde, R. A. (1990). The interdependence of the behavioral sciences [Monograph]. *Philosophical Transactions of the Royal Society, 329,* 217–277.

Kreutzer, M. A., Leonard, C., & Flavell, J. H. (1975). An interview study of children's knowledge about memory. *Monographs of the Society for Research in Child Development, 40* (Whole No. 1).

**Abstract or synopsis**

If you wish to cite the abstract of a published article rather than the article itself, provide a complete entry for the published article and cite the source of the abstract, if it is different, in parentheses. Place the designation Abstract within brackets after the title and before the period.

Dorin, J. R., Inglis, J. D., & Porteous, D. J. (1989). Selection for precise chromosomal targeting of a dominant marker by homologous recombination [Abstract]. *Science, 243,* 1357–1360. (From Science Abstracts, 1989, 75, Abstract No. 1153).

**Article in press**

When an article either is being considered or has been accepted for publication, the phrase in press takes the position of the date, and the name of the journal follows, but no volume or page numbers are given.

Smith, S. (in press). An experiment in bilingual education. *Journal of Bilingual Education.*

Two such articles by the same author should be identified with lowercase letters preceded by a hyphen: (*in press-a, in press-b*).

## Books and Chapters of Books

### Basic form

The entry for a book begins with the last name of the author, followed by a comma and the initials of the author's first names, followed by periods. The date of publication appears in parentheses, followed by a period. Only the first word of the book title, the first word of the subtitle, and proper nouns and adjectives are capitalized. The entire title and the end period are italicized. Facts of publication include the city of publication and the state, using U.S. Postal Service abbreviations (See Appendix A). Only seven American cities may be given without also including the state: Baltimore, Boston, Chicago, Los Angeles, New York, Philadelphia, and San Francisco. The city of publication is followed by a colon and the name of the publisher, in abbreviated form; however, the names of university presses are spelled out. The entry ends with a period.

> Nagel, P. C. (1992). *The Lees of Virginia: Seven generations of an American family.* NY: Oxford University Press.

### Two or more authors

For a book by more than one author, invert and list the names of all the authors. Use commas to separate surnames and initials. Place an ampersand (&) before the name of the last author.

> Forsyth, A., & Thornhill, R. (1983). *The evolution of insect mating.* Cambridge, MA: Harvard University Press.

### Brochure and Pamphlet

Treat a brochure and Pamphlet like a book, but designate it as a brochure within brackets.

### Edition other than the first

Identify an edition other than the first within parentheses following the title without any intervening punctuation. The number of the edition should be in serial form (2nd, 3rd, 4th, etc.) or, if it is a word, abbreviated (*Rev. ed.*).

> Dreyfus, H. (1989). *What computers can't do* (2nd ed.). N.Y.: Harper.

### Reprinted work

The entry for a reprinted work indicates the original date of publication within parentheses.

> Darwin, C. (1964). *On the origin of the species: A facsimile of the first edition* (Introd. Ernst Mayer). Cambridge, MA: Harvard University Press. (Original work published 1859).

The parenthetical reference in the text includes both dates: (Darwin, 1859/1964).

Treat a paperbound book issued in a year other than that of the hardcover edition as a reprinted work.

> Jamieson, N. L. (1995). *Understanding Vietnam.* Berkeley: University of California Press. (First published in hardcover 1993)

When a university press's name includes the state, it may be omitted after the city. The parenthetical reference in the text includes both dates: (Jamieson 1993/1995).

### Edited volume

Indicate that a book is an edited volume by placing the abbreviation for editor (Ed.) or editors (Eds.) within parentheses in the author position.

> Stanton, D. C. (Ed.). (1987). *The female autograph: Theory and practice of autobiography from the tenth to the twentieth century.* Chicago, IL: University of Chicago Press.

### Chapter or article in edited book

In a reference to a chapter or article in an edited book, place the name of the author of the chapter in the author position, followed by the chapter title. The second part of the entry identifies the book in which the article appears. The name(s) of the editor(s) is (are) not inverted when not at the beginning of the entry. The page numbers for the individual chapter or article appear in parentheses after the title of the book.

> Burghardt, G. M. (1984). On the origins of play. In P. K. Smith (Ed.), *Play in animals* and humans (pp. 5–42). Oxford, Eng.: Blackwell.

For two or more editors, use the abbreviation Eds.

When the author of the article and the editor of the book are the same, but the book includes articles by other authors, list the name in both the author and the editor positions.

> Olney, J. (1980). Autobiography and the cultural moment: A thematic, historical, and bibliographical introduction. In J. Olney (Ed.), *Autobiography: Essays theoretical and critical* (pp. 3–27). Princeton, NJ: Princeton University Press.

When all the chapters in a book are by the same author and you wish to cite one of them by title, place the word In before the book title. The following example indicates that Finke is the author of both the chapter and the book.

> Finke, L. (1992). The rhetoric of desire in the courtly lyric. In *Feminist Theory, Women's Writing* (pp. 29–74). Ithaca, NY: Cornell University Press.

### Reprinted article

When an article in a collection was published previously, list the version you actually used, but give the original citation in parentheses; notice the distinct listing for pages and the position of the year.

> Howarth, H. L. (1980). Some principles of autobiography. In J. Olney (Ed.), *Autobiography: Essays theoretical and critical* (pp. 84–114). Princeton, NJ: Princeton University Press. (Reprinted from *New Literary History, 5,* pp. 363–381, 1974)

The parenthetical citation in the text includes both publication dates: (Howarth, 1974/1980).

**Works without designated author**

Cite a book, brochure or pamphlet without an author or editor by title alone.

> *Guidelines and application form for directors, 1996 summer seminars for school teachers* [Brochure]. (1994). Washington, DC: National Endowment for the Humanities.

**Author as publisher**

When you consider the publisher to be the author, replace the name of the publisher with Author.

> Teachers Insurance and Annuity Association, College Retirement Equities Fund. (1995). *The participant* [Pamphlet]. NY: Author.

**Multivolume works**

For a multivolume work published over several years, place in parentheses the year of publication of the first volume and that of the last volume, separated by a hyphen.

> Ripley, C. P. (Ed.). (1985–1992). *The black abolitionist papers* (Vols. 1–5). Chapel Hill: University of North Carolina Press.

When referring to the entire multivolume work within the text, cite it as (Ripley, 1985–1992).

To refer to a single volume in a multivolume series, include only the relevant date, and place the volume number after the title without any intervening punctuation.

> Ripley, C. P. (Ed.). (1987). *The black abolitionist papers* (Vol. 2). Chapel Hill, NC: University of North Carolina Press.

When each volume has an individual title, provide both the multivolume and the volume titles, italicized continuously.

> Freehling, W. W. (1992). *Secessionists at bay, 1776–1854: Vol 1. The road to disunion.* New York: Oxford University Press.

**Translated work**

Indicate the name of a translator within parentheses after the title by the initials of the first name(s) and the full last name. If you have used only the English translation, you do not need to include the original title. If you wish to do so, place it within brackets.

> Derrida, J. (1976). *Of grammatology* (G. Spivak, Trans.). Baltimore: Johns Hopkins University Press. (Original work published 1967).

The parenthetical reference in the text should indicate the original date of publication, as well as the date of the translation: (Derrida, 1967/1976).

**Book in a foreign language**

When you cite from a book in a foreign language, supply an English translation of the original title within brackets. If the work has not been translated, use your own translation or the English title by which the work is known. The bracketed title is not italicized.

> Kristeva, J. (1983). *L'Histoires d'amour* [Tales of love]. Paris: Denoël.

**Work in a series**

The entry for an individually titled work in a series provides both the series title and volume.

> Eiser, J. R. (Ed.). (1990). *Attitudinal judgment.* Springer Series in Social Psychology, no. 11. New York: Springer-Verlag, 1990.

## Technical and Research Reports

**Basic entry**

Entries for technical and research reports should follow the basic format for a book entry. The identifying title, series, or number of the report, if any, should be placed in parentheses immediately after the title. The name of the agency publishing the report should not be abbreviated as an acronym, even if it is well known.

> Gates, J. P. (1991). *Educational and training opportunities in sustainable agriculture* (U.S. Department of Agriculture). Beltsville, MD: National Agricultural Library.

**Report from an information service**

For a report that comes from an information service, such as the National Technical Information Service (NTIS) or Educational Resources Information Center (ERIC), identify the service and document number in parentheses at the end of the entry.

> Groak, J. J. (1974). *Utilization of library resources by-students in non-residential degree programs.* Washington, DC: Government Printing Office. (ERIC Document Reproduction Service No. ED121236)

**Report from a university**

When a university (as opposed to a university press) is the publisher, provide the name of the university, followed by the name of the specific unit or department.

> Carter, G. E., Parker, J. R., & Bentley, S. (Eds.). (1984). *Minority literature and the urban experience.* Lacrosse, WI: University of Wisconsin, Institute for Minority Studies.

**Report from a corporation or organization**

American Museum of Natural History. (1995). *Annual report, 1993–1994.* New York: Author.

## Proceedings of Meetings

When a presentation at a meeting appears in book form, the entry follows the format for an article in an edited book.

> Eble, C. C. (1976). Etiquette books as linguistic authority. In P. A. Reich (Ed.), *The Second LACUS Forum, 1975* (pp. 468–475). Columbia, SC: Hornbeams.

**Unpublished paper presented at meeting**

For an unpublished paper presented at a conference or symposium, indicate the date of the presentation within parentheses after the name of the author and identify the conference as fully as necessary after the title. Include both city and state.

Jochens, J. (1992, October). Gender equality in law?: The case of medieval Iceland. Paper presented at the 26th Annual Conference of the Center for Medieval and Early Renaissance Studies, Binghamton, NY.

### Poster session

Gilbert, D. R. (1995, August). *Investigations into low temperature and low pressure deposition of diamond thin films.* Poster session presented at the Applied Diamond Conference 1995, National Institute of Standards and Technology, Gaithersburg, MD.

## Dissertations and Theses

### Microfilm of dissertation

When you use the microfilm of a dissertation as the source, give the microfilm number, as well as the volume and page numbers in *Dissertation Abstracts International.*

Baker, C. A. (1985). *Multiple alliance commitments: The role of the United States in the Falklands war. Dissertation Abstracts International, 45,* 4445B. (UMI No. 85–77, 123).

### Typescript of dissertation

When you use the typescript copy of a dissertation, give the university and year, as well as the volume and page numbers in *Dissertation Abstracts International.* If the dates are different, provide the date of the dissertation after the name of the university.

Moskop, W. W. (1995). The prudent politician: An extension of Aristotle's ethical theory (Doctoral dissertation, George Washington University, 1984). *Dissertation Abstracts International, 45,* 4445B.

When the years are different list them chronologically, separated by a slash, in the parenthetical reference: (Moskop, 1984/1995).

### Unpublished dissertation or thesis

Treat a dissertation or thesis that does not appear in *Dissertation Abstracts International* as an unpublished work. Italicize the title and identify the university, the city, and the state (if it is not part of the university's name).

Peters, B. (1995). *The biographer as autobiographer: The case of Virginia Woolf.* Unpublished master's thesis, Pace University, Riverdale, NY.

## Unpublished Materials and Works of Limited Circulation

### Completed material not submitted for publication

When unpublished material is in completed form, italicize the title and indicate the unpublished status at the end of the entry.

Johnson, S. J. (1992). *The teaching of twelfth-grade advanced placement mathematics.* Unpublished manuscript, University of California, San Diego.

**Manuscript accepted for publication**

When an unpublished manuscript has been accepted for publication, designate it as in press.

> Little., C. A. (1992). *Forms of childhood autism.* In press.

**Draft material**

When you refer to unpublished material in unfinished form, such as a rough draft or unorganized tabular data, put the name of the topic in brackets in the title position without italics. Indicate the status of the material at the end of the entry. Use the date you consulted the material.

> Jensen, H. C. (1992). [Settlement patterns for Norwegian immigrants, 1890–1920]. Unpublished raw data.

**Publication of limited circulation**

When a work, although published, probably will not be available in most libraries, give the address at which a copy might be located or obtained.

> Inouye, L. (1993, April). GECA-The organic agriculture training school, El Salvador. *Oxfam American project report,* pp. 1–4. [Brochure]. (Available from Oxfam America, 26 West Street, Boston, MA 02111–1206).

**Reviews and Published Interviews**

**Book review**

Provide the title of the book under review within brackets following the title.

> Moore, W. (1992, October 11). Great physicist, great guy [Review of the book *Genius: The life and science of Richard Feynman*]. *The New York Times Book Review,* p. 3.

If the review does not have a title, use the material within brackets as the title, retaining the brackets.

> Kienitz, G. M. (1992). [Review of the book *Tennyson and the doom of Romanticism*]. *Religion and Literature, 24*(1), 87–90.

**Film or video program review**

Provide the title of the film or video program under review within brackets following the title. If the review does not have a title, use the material within brackets as the title, retaining the brackets, as shown previously for a book.

> Canby, V. (1992, May 22). Cruise and Kidman in old-fashioned epic [Review of the motion picture *Far and away*]. *The New York Times,* p. C10.

**Published interview**

Follow the basic format appropriate for the book or periodical in which the interview is published. The name of the interviewer occupies the place of the author, and the person interviewed is identified by both first and last names within brackets.

> Jahanbegloo, R. (1992, May 28). Philosophy and life [Interview with Isaiah Berlin]. *The New York Review of Books,* pp. 46–54.

Unpublished interviews conducted in person or through media such as telephone or e-mail are cited parenthetically within the text as personal communications but are not listed as references.

## Audiovisual Media

In entries for audiovisual media, place the name of the principal organizer or creator in the author position, and in parentheses identify the person's function. The nature of the medium should be indicated in brackets immediately after the title. Enter the date and place of publication as for a book. If a work has limited circulation, provide an address from which it can be obtained.

### Motion picture

Include information about contributors within brackets; also note that instead of a city-state notation, only the country is given.

> Eastwood, C. (Director). (1992). *Unforgiven* [Motion picture]. [With Clint Eastwood, Gene Hackman, and Morgan Freeman]. United States: Warner Brothers.

> Batty, P. (Producer). (1987). *The divided Union* [Video]. United States: Fusion Video.

### Television broadcast

Entries for television series place the name of the producer in the author position. For an individual episode of a series or a single program, place the name of the writer or reporter in the author position and place the name of the producer in the position of the editor. Also note that the broadcasting company's name is spelled out in full.

### Television series

> Moyers, B. (Writer and producer). (1995). *The language of life* [Television series]. Newark, NJ: Public Broadcasting Service.

### Single episode from series

> Jennings, P. (1995, July 27). Hiroshima: Why the bomb was dropped [Television series episode]. In Peter *Jennings reporting* (D. Gelber and M. Smith,producers). New York: American Broadcasting Company.

### Individual program

> Lacy, M. D. (1995, September 4). *Richard Wright: Black boy* (G. P. Land and J. Judin, Executive Producers, Independent Television Service and Mississippi Educational Television). New York: Public. Broadcasting Service.

### Recording

Entries for recordings begin with the writer of the composition, followed by the original date.

> Handel, G. F. (1771). Suite no. 1 in F major [Cond. N. Marriner, Academy of St. Martin-in-the-Fields]. On *Water music/Wassermusik* [CD]. Hayes, Middlesex, Eng. : EMI. (1989)

> Williams, M. (1971). Katydid's ditty [Recorded by Mannheim Steamroller]. On *Classical gas* [CD]. Omaha, NE: American Gramaphone Records. (1987)

**CD**

When you have a number for a CD or other material, include it with the description, enclosed in parentheses.

> Hunter, K. (Speaker). (1989). *Family counseling* (Audiocassette Recording No. 1175). Washington, DC: American Psychological Association.

> Westen, D. (Author and speaker). (1995). *Is anyone really normal? Perspectives on abnormal psychology* (Videocassette No. 658). Springfield, VA: Teaching Company.

**The List of References**

In APA style, the list of sources is entitled "References." This list should be confined to those works that are actually cited within the article, report, or dissertation, and it must include all of the cited works. If you wish to provide a list of additional readings or the full range of works that you consulted, you may do so in a bibliographical appendix (not acceptable for an article to be submitted to an APA journal).

**Order of entries**

Entries appear in alphabetical order according to the last name of the author or, if there is no author, the first word in the title, excluding articles.

**Two or more works by same author**

Two or more works by the same author appear in chronological order by date of publication, beginning with the earliest.

> Jones, J. J. (2005).
> Jones, J. J. (2006).

Two or more works by the same author and with the same publication date appear in alphabetical order by title and are identified by serial lowercase letters after the date. Repeat the name of the author in each entry.

> Jones, J. J. (2005a). Breakdown in communication....
> Jones, J. J. (2005b). Businesses organize....

One-author entries precede two-author entries beginning with the same author, even if the publication date is later; two-author entries precede three-author entries, and so on.

> Jones, J. J. (2005).
> Jones, J. J., & Smith, S. S. (2002).

Sources with the same first author are alphabetized by the surname of the second author. If the first two names are the same, alphabetize by the third author, and so on.

> Jones, J. J., Smith, S. S., & Adams, A. A. (2004).
> Jones, J. J., Smith, S. S. & Bentley, B. B. (2001).

An author entry precedes an entry for the same person as an editor, which precedes an entry for the same person as a coauthor or coeditor.

> Jones, J. J. (2005).
> Jones, J. J. (Ed.) (2005).
> Jones, J. J., & Smith, S. S. (2005).
> Jones, J. J., & Smith, S. S. (Eds.) (2005).

### Different authors with same surname

Authors with the same surname should be alphabetized by the initial of the first name.

> Jones, J. J. (2005).
> Jones, M. J. (2005).

### Anonymous work

For a work explicitly identified as anonymous, use the word Anonymous as the author entry and alphabetize accordingly.

> Anonymous. (1996). *Primary Colors*. NY: Random.

### Legal citation

Place citations for legal documents in the reference list (not at the bottom of the page as in legal documents and periodicals). Enter them without italics, and alphabetize them by the first significant word in the entry.

> Jones v. Smith, Volume, Source, Page (Court Date).
> Smith v. Jones, Volume, Source, Page (Court Date).

# References

Alloy, L. B. & Tabachnik, N. (1984). Assessment of covariation by humans and animals: The joint influence of prior expectations and current situational information. *Psychological Review, 91,* 112–149.

Bandura, A. (Ed.). (1995). *Self-efficacy in changing societies.* NY: Cambridge University Press.

Bargh, J. A. (1996). *Automaticity in social psychology. Social psychology: Handbook of basic principles.* NY: Guilford.

Bohner, G., Bless, H., Schwarz, N., & Strack, F. (1998). What triggers causal attributions? The impact of valence and subjective probability. *European Journal of Social Psychology, 18,* 335–345.

Boninger, D. S., Gleicher, F., & Strathman, A. (1994). Counterfactual thinking: From what might have been to what may be. *Journal of Personality and Social Psychology, 67,* 297–307.

Bouts, P., Spears, R., & Van de Pligt, J. (1992). Counterfactual processing and the correspondence between events and outcomes: Normality versus value. *European Journal of Social Psychology, 22,* 387–396.

Branscombe, N. R., Crosby, P., & Weir, J. A. (1993). Social inferences concerning male and female homeowners who use a gun to shoot an intruder. *Aggressive Behavior, 19,* 113–124.

## Appendix A

**Abbreviations of State Names**

In Chicago style and MLA, the name of the city is often all that is needed to identify the place of publication in a note or a bibliographical reference. When one city might be confused with another (such as Lexington, Kentucky, and Lexington, Massachusetts) or if the location of a city is not well known, include the name of the state or territory, using abbreviations. In contrast, APA requires that states be listed with all U. S. cities except Baltimore, Boston, Chicago, Los Angeles, New York, Philadelphia, and San Francisco.

Use these abbreviations only in bibliographical references or in tables; do not use them in the text.

| STATE NAME | U.S. POSTAL SERVICE ABBREVIATION (APA, MLA, AND CHICAGO MANUALS) | TRADITIONAL ABBREVIATION (LEGAL CITATIONS) |
|---|---|---|
| Alabama | AL | Ala. |
| Alaska | AK | Alaska |
| American Samoa | AS | Amer. Samoa |
| Arizona | AZ | Ariz. |
| Arkansas | AR | Ark. |
| California | CA | Calif. |
| Canal Zone | CZ | C.Z. |
| Colorado | CO | Colo. |
| Connecticut | CT | Conn. |
| Delaware | DE | Del. |
| District of Columbia | DC | D.C. |
| Florida | FL | Fla. |
| Georgia | GA | Ga. |
| Guam | GU | Guam |
| Hawaii | HI | Hawaii |
| Idaho | ID | Idaho |
| Illinois | IL | Ill. |
| Indiana | IN | Ind. |
| Iowa | IA | Iowa |
| Kansas | KS | Kans. |
| Kentucky | KY | Ky. |
| Louisiana | LA | La. |
| Maine | ME | Maine |
| Maryland | MD | Md. |
| Massachusetts | MA | Mass. |
| Michigan | MI | Mich. |

| STATE NAME | U.S. POSTAL SERVICE ABBREVIATION (APA, MLA, AND CHICAGO MANUALS) | TRADITIONAL ABBREVIATION (LEGAL CITATIONS) |
| --- | --- | --- |
| Minnesota | MN | Minn. |
| Mississippi | MS | Miss. |
| Missouri | MO | Mo. |
| Montana | MT | Mont. |
| Nebraska | NE | Nebr. |
| Nevada | NV | Nev. |
| New Hampshire | NH | N.H. |
| New Jersey | NJ | N.J. |
| New Mexico | NM | N.Mex. |
| New York | NY | N.Y. |
| North Carolina | NC | N.C. |
| North Dakota | ND | N.Dak. |
| Ohio | OH | Ohio |
| Oklahoma | OK | Okla. |
| Oregon | OR | Oreg. |
| Pennsylvania | PA | Pa. |
| Puerto Rico | PR | P.R. |
| Rhode Island | RI | R.I. |
| South Carolina | SC | S.C. |
| South Dakota | SD | S.Dak. |
| Tennessee | TN | Tenn. |
| Texas | TX | Tex. |
| Utah | UT | Utah |
| Vermont | VT | Vt. |
| Virginia | VA | Va. |
| Virgin Islands | VI | V.I. |
| Washington | WA | Wash. |
| West Virginia | WV | W.Va. |
| Wisconsin | WI | Wis. |
| Wyoming | WY | Wyo. |

# STUDENT SAMPLE RESEARCH PAPERS

# Nursing

Dr. Denise Lagos
English 112 or English 101
Career Research Paper

Rommel Magallanes
Month Year

# TABLE OF CONTENTS

# 1. Introduction

Nursing is a diverse and interesting field for a profession. It is one of the most respected in all health care occupations. Post (1999) explains that nursing care is not new; in fact, "Care for the ill or injured has existed since the beginning of recorded history, but modern nursing began in the nineteenth century with Florence Nightingale (1820–1910). Before Nightingale, there were no professional nurses. When people were sick, they relied on family members or friends for care" (p. 1). George (2002) considers Nightingale as the mother of modern nursing because she was able to put all her experiences together in her life to help her in the development of modern nursing.

Nurses are considered the backbone of the health care industry. Nurses have direct contact with patients. Nurses are the ones who directly show tender loving care to the sick, ill, and injured. According to Post (1999),

> Nightingale thought of nursing as a calling instead of a profession, because she was a religious woman who believed that nurses were called by God to care for others. She wanted to make it clear that to her, nursing was a moral and religious act, not simply a medical one. In fact,

1

she emphasized caring over science. She believed that good nursing care fulfilled the nurse's moral obligation to care for others by putting the patient in the best condition for nature to act upon him (p. 1).

Nowadays, treatment of some illnesses seems to be very easy and fast because of all the advancements in technology. To mention some, we have advanced laser surgeries, organ transplants, dialysis, and more. But, treatment and successful operation are not the only solution for every injury or illness. As humans, we must not forget that patients are still longing for the human care and affection after each successful treatment and operation. Patients most importantly need the compassion, empathy, and the tender loving care of nurses.

# 2. Subfields and Specializations

Registered nurses can specialize in one or more areas of patient care. There generally are four ways to specialize. Registered nurses can choose a particular work setting or type of treatment, such as preoperative nurses, who work in operating rooms and assist surgeons. Registered nurses also may choose to specialize in specific health conditions, as do diabetes management nurses, who assist patients to manage diabetes. Other registered nurses specialize in working with one or more organs or body system types, such as dermatology nurses, who work with patients who have skin disorders. Registered nurses also can choose to work in a well-defined population, such as geriatric nurses, who work with the elderly. Some registered nurses may combine specialties. For example, pediatric oncology nurses deal with children and adolescents who have cancer (Bureau of Labor Statistics [BLS], 2008, pp. 1–2).

The nursing field is one of the most diverse of all health care professions. There are a wide range of areas for nurses when it comes to deciding what to specialize in.

Nurses who are tired of doing bedside care in large hospitals may have an option to practice their profession as private and establish their own nursing home. Some may even work as a school nurse or as a community nurse. Others prefer to be a flight or a corporate nurse.

# 3. Employment Opportunities and Salary

Employment opportunities for registered nurses exist with a wide range and variety. In fact, employment for registered nurses grows faster than any other field of occupations. The shortage of nurses in the country will surely give anyone pursuing the course a good chance of a stable employment (White, 2002).

Shortage in registered nurses is very obvious nowadays. One good proof is the vast recruitment of foreign nurses. According to the BLS (2008), "Overall job opportunities for registered nurses are expected to be excellent, but may vary by employment and geographic setting. Employment for RNs is expected to grow much faster than the average for all occupations through 2016, and, because the occupation is very large, many new jobs will result. In fact, registered nurses are projected to generate 587,000 new jobs, among the largest number of new jobs for any occupation" (p. 6).

With regards to salary, the nursing career is very lucrative. In an article, O'Brien (2008) indicates that nurses' average salary is almost $59,650 in 2007. Salary is determined by factors such as education and experience. The more advanced in studies, learning, and experience, the more chances of having a better position and higher salary. Aside from having a good base salary, nurses are offered good benefit packages. One of the good benefits is having a differential pay. Holidays and graveyard shifts pay even more differential pay.

According to the BLS (2008), "Median annual earnings of registered nurses were $57,280 in May 2006. The middle fifty percent earned between $47,710 and $69,850. The lowest ten percent earned less than $40,250, and the highest 10 percent earned more than $83,440" (p. 8).

All in all, the salary is determined on the level of education earned, the years of experience, and through the expertise in the field of specialization. Nowadays, critical areas even pay much higher than any other areas of patient care (Communication).

# 4. Advantages and Disadvantages

The nursing career is a very interesting field as a profession. Aside from various interests of specialization to train in, there is always a room and desire for continuous learning. Because people want to always feel better, people are also trying to discover new things and better ways to survive in this world. Patients are not the only people who are benefiting from the nurses, but immediate families are as well. Having the tender loving care of a nurse is not only delivered to the sick patients, but also this type of care is extended to close relatives and friends.

5

Liability is one of the disadvantages in the nursing career (Communication). Nurses are held accountable for the treatment given to their patients. Dealing with patients is not a joke. It has to be taken seriously and in a gentle way. The process of dealing with a patient is also dealing with a precious life. According to Post (1999), "Accountability is a basic moral value and moral foundation in nursing. Nurses are accountable for their work. This means they are personally responsible for what they do, and they are expected to be able to give good reasons for their nursing decisions and actions" (p. 6).

# 5. Interview Data

The researcher had the chance to interview an emergency room nurse. The interviewee already worked as a nurse for more than fifteen years in various hospitals and health care facilities. Based on her education, training, and experience, the respondent was the perfect example of a nurse in the nursing field.

The respondent shared and discussed most of her experiences as she journeyed into her nursing career. She mentioned that nursing is a diverse career. There are a lot of specialization areas to choose from. Areas of specialization are the emergency rooms, intensive care units, pediatric wards, medical and surgical wards, special and critical units, and more. Additionally, the interviewee indicated that nurses can also work outside hospital care by being a community nurse, school nurse, flight nurse, corporate nurse, and more. Another area of opportunity is the nursing entrepreneurship. Nurses who have enough knowledge, training, and work experience can establish their own nursing home and private duty work. The professional indicated that unemployment is never a problem in the nursing career. As projected in the news, there will be shortages in nursing in the future (Communication).

Aside from mentioning that the nursing career is very lucrative, a lot of good benefit packages are available when applying for a job in the health care industry. The nursing career is very fulfilling for the informant because she loves what she is doing. The nursing profession for her is a job that drives her to go to work every day.

The interviewee illustrated how a professional can grow in the nursing career. The respondent indicated that there are a lot of chances to go up the ladder. Given the right education, training, and experience, there will always be room for promotion. But, most of all, the professional reiterated that the love, care, compassion, and empathy for patients are the most important things to be learned in heart and in mind in order to be a successful nurse.

The research and interview data gathered by the researcher confirms that the nursing profession is an appealing, wise, and excellent career to pursue.

# 6. Conclusion

Nursing is a diverse and very interesting profession. The wide range of specialization areas opens a lot of opportunity for anyone who wants to pursue this career. Aside from having lucrative and competitive wages, good health care and family benefit packages also await the nurse. However, excellent compensation in the nursing career is not the only reason for pursuing this career. The love of the work is more important. For some, the fulfillment of caring for others is far more rewarding.

Anyone interested in pursuing the nursing career should also be prepared to accept challenges. Nursing is a continuous process. There are no dead ends. Anyone interested in becoming a registered nurse must be willing and interested in learning new things every now and then, because new sophisticated procedures and equipment are continuously being discovered in making the health of others better. Additionally, having the ability and willingness to be a part of a team is necessary, because teamwork is an important aspect in health care.

According to Ingles (as quoted by Frederickson, 2003), "Nursing is the art of helping people feel better" (p. 6). Anyone interested in the career of nursing must be willing to work and deal with people who may be depressed or irritable because of their illnesses and health problems. Compassion, empathy, tender loving care, and, most of all, patience are the qualities needed by anyone who wants to pursue a health care career.

# References

Bureau of Labor Statistics, U.S. Department of Labor. (2008). *Occupational outlook handbook.* Registered Nurses.

Frederickson, K. (2003). *Opportunities in nursing careers.* New York, NY: McGraw-Hill Companies.

George, J. (Ed.). (2002). *Nursing theories: The base for professional nursing practice.* New Jersey: Pearson Education.

O'Brien, A. (2008). Salary survey 2008. *Advance for Nurses, 8*(4), 9.

Post, S. (Ed.). (1999). *Nursing-bioethics for students.* New York, NY: Macmillan.

White, L. (2002). *Career success in nursing.* Canada: Delmar.

# Automotive Collision Repair Technician

Dr. Denise Lagos
English 112 or English 101
Career Research Paper

Daniel Zielinski
Month Year

# TABLE OF CONTENTS

# 1. Interest

The researcher has been passionate about cars since he was a young boy. He always had many toy cars in his room. When he got bored with them, he used to take his mother's nail polish and repaint his little cars, so they looked different. As he was getting older, he became more interested in working on cars. At the age of ten, the researcher loved to spend time watching television shows about men who rebuilt old damaged cars into new, shining cars. In the year 2001, when the ethnographer saw the movie "The Fast and the Furious" for the first time, he was inspired and became interested in cars even more. He liked the way the cars in the movie were made. Custom body kits, rims, and the new, shiny paint of the cars impressed him. Since that time, he has always dreamed about rebuilding cars, making them look like the cars from the movie.

When the researcher was in the ninth grade, his parents had bought him a used moped. The moped had a lot of plastic pieces that covered mechanical parts of the bike. Most of the pieces had many scratches and cracks due to the usage by the previous owner. One day he decided to work on that used, dilapidated moped and made it look brand new. He went to the garage where he kept his moped and took off all of the parts that covered it. He saw somewhere on television that people used fiberglass and car body filler to repair broken parts of a car, so he went to a store and bought all the necessary materials he needed. When he got back to the garage, he started working on those pieces that required the most time to fix. It was his first time using fiberglass, so at the beginning, his work appeared rather sloppy. But after a few hours, he did really well. The next day he had to sand the spots where he put fiberglass on. Then he used car body filler to cover all of the cracks and deep scratches, and made the surface smooth. When the body filler had dried, he had to sand the surface very carefully. Sanding is not an easy process, it took the ethnographer a while, but when he was finally done, he was excited. The last step was painting. It was definitely his favorite part of the job because the new paint changed the whole appearance of the moped. The painting was really difficult. He had to be very careful and accurate. When the researcher had finally completed the work, the moped was shiny and looked like it had just come out of the factory.

The next day when his friends saw the moped, they were impressed and asked him who had done the work. The ethnographer was very proud when he said that he had done all of the work by himself. Later, when his father saw the moped, he told his son that he liked the "new" moped and that he was proud of him because he did a really good job. This experience gave the researcher a great sense of pride because of what he had accomplished.

# 2. Educational Requirements

The three educational requirements for a collision repair technician are high school, postsecondary training, and certification and licensing. Very often a high school diploma or GED is the first basic requirement to start the occupation. While in high school, students should focus and pay a lot of attention in classes such as reading, math, and computer science. Improving reading skills will definitely be helpful in understanding different types of technical manuals. Basic math and computer science are required to calculate the right adjustments in order to restore the car into its original shape (Ferguson, 2010).

3

There is no formal training required to start working as a collision repair technician. Some employers decide to hire people with no formal training and offer them hands on training. However, most employers would rather hire someone with an education in collision repair than someone without formal training at all. Those students who have completed vocational or technical schools, have a better opportunity for a salary increase and promotions (Communication).

Nguyen (2000) indicates that in the United States of America, there are about 1,420 postsecondary schools that specialize in collision repair programs. While attending these schools, students take courses in different parts of the field. The most popular courses to take are structural analysis and damage repair, mechanical and electrical components, plastics and adhesives, and refinishing and painting. Nowadays, collision repair has become more technical than in the past. Therefore, academic courses such as English, math, communications, science, and chemistry are often required to take along with technical courses (Ferguson, 2010).

Additional certification or licensing is optional. However, it is a great recognition for being successful in the field of collision repair. The National Institute for Automotive Service Excellence (ASE) offers the certification for collision repair technicians. In order to be certified, the technician has to pass a written exam and have at least two years of experience working in the field. Postsecondary school is often counted as one year of the experience. The exams are divided into four categories: structural analysis and damage repair, mechanical and electrical components, plastics and adhesives, and refinishing and painting. Technicians can choose how many exams to take. Those who pass at least one of the tests earn ASE certification. In order to become an ASE master collision repair and refinish technician, a student has to pass all four tests. In order to keep their certification, technicians must retake the exams every five years (Ferguson, 2010).

# 3. Employment

Automotive repair technicians have a few different opportunities to choose in their career. They can decide whether to work for a private auto repair shop, dealership, car rental company, or start their own business.

> Automotive body and related repairers held about 185,900 jobs in 2008; about 10 percent specialized in automotive glass installation and repair. Around 62 percent of repairers worked for automotive repair and maintenance shops, while 17 percent worked for automobile dealers. A small number worked for wholesalers of motor vehicles, parts, and supplies. About 12 percent of automotive body repairers were self-employed (BLS, 2009, p. 2).

Demand for collision repair technicians seems to have increased somewhat from 2008 (BLS, 2009). Each year, the number of the cars on the road increases. Manufacturers produce more cars. Along with increasing the number of cars on the roads, accident rates will go up as well. More car accidents mean that there will be more work for a collision repair technician. Technology used to make new cars keeps changing from year to year. New cars are made out of plastics, aluminum, and steel alloys. Each of them requires a different type of work. Therefore, there will be a high demand for most knowledgeable and up-to-date technicians (Ferguson, 2010).

In a 2003 article, Healey emphasizes that the number of cars made of aluminum is increasing, yet there are not enough technicians who are trained to repair aluminum parts. People with formal training and certification in automotive collision repair will have the best opportunities to get the best job. People without formal training will definitely struggle with the competition in the field, and it may be difficult to get a job.

# 4. Salary/Benefits

Salary for automotive collision technicians often varies. It depends on a few factors such as geographic location of the workplace, experience of the technician, and the type of shop you work in (Ferguson, 2010). Location of the work place plays an important role in the salary a technician earns. Some areas have a higher demand for collision repairers than others. "Top-paying states are Colorado (average $23.83/hour), Alaska ($20.68), and Nevada ($20.52)" (Kennedy, p. 2).

Education, formal training, and certifications are other factors that decide on the income collision repairers earn. People without any knowledge or formal training almost always start as helpers (Communication). BLS

(2009) stated, "Helpers and trainees typically earn between 30 percent and

60 percent of the earning of skilled workers. They are paid hourly until they

are skilled enough to be paid on an incentive basis" (p. 3). Skilled technicians

who work for automotive dealers or body shops usually get incentive pay

that is based on the amount of work done. Although some of the employers

often offer minimum weekly pay for their workers.

> Median hourly wages of automotive body and related repairers in-
> cluding incentive pay were $17.81 in May 2008. The middle 50 percent
> earned between $13.74 and $23.57 an hour. The lowest 10 percent
> earned less than $10.75, and the highest 10 percent earned more
> than $30.17 an hour. Median hourly wages of automotive body
> and related repairers were $18.95 in automobile dealers and $17.40
> in automotive repair and maintenance (BLS, 2010, p. 2).

Options for benefits for collision repairers are often different in each work place

and usually depend on the employer. However, health insurance and paid vaca-

tion are almost always offered to the employees. Some additional benefits that

may be available for the workers are dental and eye care as well as a pension

plan. Some employers decide to pay for an employee's certification trainings.

Sometimes when the business does well, the owner offers some bonuses to its workers (Ferguson, 2010).

# 5. Work Conditions

According to Weber (2001), most collision repair technicians work by themselves rather than in groups. However, in large shops, they work as a group. Each technician specializes in one area of the repair, such as frame or fender straightening. All of the work is performed indoors. Repairers are required to work in uncomfortable positions, which make the work difficult and painful. Even though most shops are almost always well-ventilated, the conditions are often dusty. The automotive body shop is definitely a noisy place. The noise made by sanding tools is almost always endless. Chances of getting injured are high. The most common type of injury is a cut from jagged metal. Burns from torches and heated metal are also very common. However, most technicians learn how to avoid most injuries and make their job safer (p. 38).

9

Collision repairers who perform painting jobs are exposed to very harmful fumes from the paints and solvents.

> The painter is exposed to this overspray and solvent vapors that evaporate from the overspray and the painted surface. The paint's components pose health hazards to the painter. Exposure to organic solvents affects the central nervous system. However, solvent exposures during autobody repair operations generally are reported to be below recommended exposure limits. In addition, some paints contain toxic metals such as lead and chromium. Also, polyisocyanates (which are used to obtain hard, durable surfaces) are frequently used in clear coats. Frequently used polyisocyanates are the isocyanurate trimer or the biuret of 1,6-hexamethylene diisocyanate. Exposures to these HDI-based polyisocyanates are reported to cause skin and eye irritation, respiratory sensitization, asthma, and reduced lung function (Heitbrink, Wallace, Bryant, & Ruch, 1995, p. 1023).

In order to protect themselves from the hazards of the job, technicians use professional equipment such as respirators and special types of clothing. Painters work in rooms that are designed for painting jobs. The rooms are equipped in advanced with ventilation systems to lower the painter's exposure to fumes (Communication).

# 6. Interview Data

The researcher conducted an interview with an automotive collision repair technician to learn more about the profession. The respondent was more than pleased to answer all of the questions asked by the interviewer. The informant is a certified collision repair technician and has been working in the field for over ten years.

The professional has always liked fixing cars. At the beginning, when he was hired for his first job, he started as a helper, washing and preparing cars for painting. Day after day, he gained new experiences and that was how he worked his way up and became a certified technician. He took several I-CAR classes as training in electrics, structural analysis, body repair, and more. His favorite classes were structural damage and frame repair. He claimed that I-CAR certification is really important, because without it, a repairer can only do work on an entry level. When the damage is more complicated, proper certification and knowledge is needed in order for the technician to be able to fix the problem.

The interviewee explained the process of car repair that is not as simple as it looks. First of all, estimators look at the car damage and take some notes. The damages get inspected as the estimators write the estimate of the repair and send it to an insurance company. Then parts needed for the repair are ordered, and the process of the repair begins. First, the car's structural

11

damages get fixed. This means that all the damages in the car frame are fixed to match all of the factory specifications of the car. Then all the dents in the body of the car get fixed, and the car is sent to the painting department. After the car is painted, it is ready for the final assembly.

The respondent stressed that repairing cars is a very hard job. He said that back injuries are very common and a dangerous problem in this profession. At the beginning, it is not really noticeable. However, after thirty years of hard work in this field, it can cause many types of back problems. By the conclusion of the interview, the informant suggested that the researcher find a different career and did not recommend that the researcher pursue this field. The ethnographer was surprised to hear this, yet he decided that he really wants to be a collision repair technician. The researcher will continue his pursuit in becoming an automotive collision repair technician.

# 7. Conclusion

An automotive collision repair technician's job is to fix cars that unfortunately were involved in an accident and as a result got damaged. Nowadays, car accidents are a very common problem. Everyday thousands of cars get damaged. Sometimes they are damaged significantly and cannot be repaired. However, most of the time, a collision repair technician is able to fix all of the damage and make the car look as though it just came out of the factory.

Technicians with formal experience and the right certification should easily find a job or open their own small business. With a few years of experience, the annual salary for a collision repair technician is pretty good. Additionally, benefits such as health insurance and paid vacations are big pluses. Automotive collision repair is not an easy job. However, those people who are passionate about cars and love to spend time working on them will definitely like this job.

# References

Automobile Collision Repairers. (2010). *Ferguson's career guidance center*.

Healey, J. R. (2003, July 2). Not all cars are made of steel. *USA Today*, p. B3.

Kennedy, G. M. (2010). Body repair technician. *Ferguson's Career Guidance Center*.

Nguyen, T. (2000, January). Collision repair: Smart training for smart people for a smart career. *Tech Directions, 26*.

U.S. Department of Labor. Bureau of Labor Statistics. (2010). *Automotive body and related repairers. Occupational outlook handbook*. Washington, DC: U.S. Government Printing Office.

Weber, R. M. (2001). *Opportunities in automotive service careers*. New York, NY: McGraw-Hill Companies.

# Hospitality Management

Dr. Denise Lagos
English 112 or English 101
Career Research Paper

Andrea Oviedo
Month Year

# TABLE OF CONTENTS

# 1. Background

The researcher was born in Costa Rica, which is a wonderful country with tropical weather. Any way you look at it; Costa Rica offers the best of nature's beauty and bounty. And once you are there, you can in just a very short trip, experience both the Pacific and the Caribbean coasts, each offering an entirely different world and landscape. In a 2009 article *Conde Nast Traveler,* "Costa Rica not only offers an action packed vacation, but people can easily relax in one of Costa Rica's many hot springs, indulge in a healing mud bath, or enjoy a breathtaking view of the Arenal volcano at night" (p. 10).

Medical tourism is taking off; more Americans are going abroad for medical care (vacation included). In a 2009 article, Rosenthal indicated with health care cost rising at 6% a year since 2000, and more workers losing their jobs, and health insurance experts predict that more Americans will travel abroad for medical procedures. Stephano (in Rosenthal, 2009) states, "The

Medical Tourism Association included Costa Rica in the greatest numbers of surgical trips, people can get there orthopedic surgery, spinal surgery, liposuction, and other cosmetic procedures with a side trip such as the canopy tour high above the forest floor of the Monteverde cloud forest" (p. 13). Costa Rica offers great vacation plans with highly qualified professionals in the industry.

When the interviewer was a young girl, she used to go with her sister on vacations and visited some of the incredible places in her country. For her, one of the most memorable days was when she was twelve years old and she and her sister's family went to a hotel called Brisas del Pacifico in Costa Rica. The researcher had never been to such a place. That day they arrived at night and everything seemed to be good, but when she woke up, she had the most incredible feeling. She was waking up by the ocean as waves were hitting the beach, as soon as she heard that, she got up and saw the beautiful view in front of her, it was stunning. The blue of the ocean, the fresh breeze, the beautiful garden, and the landscape in general were amazing. Years passed, and she continued traveling around her country.

When the ethnographer was twenty years old, she had a great opportunity to start working in the International Airport in Costa Rica. Working in the airport, the researcher had a great chance to meet people from all over the world and stay in contact with different cultures; there her passion for hospitality management grew and her interest for learning more about cultures grew as well. The comments that people made about the wonders of her country made her feel very proud of her roots and confirm that the beauty of her country was very vast and her dream of having a career and a great time was possible. After three years of working at the international airport, the interviewer thought about expanding her horizons, so she decided to go to the United States of America to learn English and learn about the American culture.

Luckily for the interviewer, coming to the United States of America has been a wonderful opportunity to learn. Here she has worked in the hospitality area such as restaurant, and she had to interact with people from all around the world. Additionally, she has worked for families and learned about cultures such as Chinese and Hindu. The interviewer is in this career because she has had experience in the service industry with very positive feedback, and she would like to be part of the labor force of her country. Additionally, the researcher wants to take all the knowledge and skills that she can learn in the United States, and practice in Costa Rica as a professional to continue admiring the beauty of her country. With time, the ethnographer would like to own and run her own business.

# 2. Concept

The hospitality industry is the largest single employer in New Jersey and one of the largest and most important industries in the new global economy. (Union County College, Hospitality Management Program [brochure]). Additionally, the hospitality and tourism industry are frequently a necessary first step in the development of emerging nations. "Hospitality not only includes hotels and restaurants, but also refers to other kinds of institutions that offer shelter, food, or both to people away from their homes." We can also expand this definition, as many people have, to include those institutions that provide other types of services to people away from home. This

4

might include private clubs, casinos, resorts, attractions such as amusements parks and so on" (Powers & Barrows, 2006, p. 5).

It is really important when we go to a place and feel that we are welcome and comfortable; that is the whole concept in the hospitality industry and the people that make that possible. Because hospitality encompasses many areas, today, managers and supervisors, as well as skilled employees, find that opportunities for advancement often mean moving from one area of the hospitality industry to another. Powers and Barrows (2006) stated that the Holiday Inns are in the hotel business, but they are also one of the largest food service companies in the United States of America. People can choose to work in different sectors of hospitality. But how important is Hospitality in the global market? "Hospitality and tourism industry contributes in excess of 5% of the gross domestic product in the United States and employs more people than the agricultural, electronics, steel, and textile industries combined. On a worldwide basis, the industry generates in excess $3.5 trillion in annual revenues and employs over 112 million people. Plus the hospitality and tourism industry contributes, on average, about 5.5 of the gross national products of countries around the world"

(Riegel & Dallas, 1998, p. 1).

# 3. Job Requirements

Depending on the company needs and the job that a person is requesting,

most entry-level jobs require little or no previous training; basic tasks

usually can be learned in a short time. For people who are still in school

and are considering this career, they can start taking subjects in business,

mathematics, and public speaking.

With some companies, people can start as the front desk help or bellman

or even as a dishwasher, and from there, can start promoting themselves,

and in time, with hard work, get a better position. "Many companies now

require management trainees to have a minimum of a bachelor's degree in

hotel and restaurant management. Many hotels and motels will also consider

candidates with liberal arts degrees in such fields as business management

and public relations if they are highly qualified and talented" (*Encyclopedia*

*of Careers*, 2003, p. 365). Many hotels fill first-level manager positions by promoting staff from within, particularly those with good communication skills, knowledge of basic computer, knowledge of management, a solid background, tact, loyalty and capacity to endure hard work, long hours, and with a good work ethic. Other very important requirements that managers and owners are looking for in target employee are: a neat person, clean appearance, and pleasant manner. A front desk job is really important because it is the first impression a guest has about the establishment, so people covering this position has to present themselves very well.

Empowerment is a really important concept in this kind of business, because how good a person is, depends on their responses to customers. Employees must be self-motivated and have initiative.

## 4. Earnings/Employers

Salary figures vary according to the worker's level of expertise, the lodging establishment, the duties involved, the size of the hotel or motel, and the location. Salary range is from $23,580 to $79,410 (Ferguson, 2011).

It is also important to note that managers may receive bonuses plus their basic salary; they can also have the opportunity to travel if the hotel is part of a hotel chain. "Managers receive paid vacation and sick days and other benefits, such as medical and life insurance, and pension or profit sharing plans. They additionally may receive free or discounted lodging, meals, parking and laundry as well as financial assistance in education" (Ferguson, 2011 p. 4).

This kind of industry is expanded every time more and more people want to be part of the business. "There are approximately fifty-eight thousand hotel and motel managers working in the United States. Forty-five percent of these workers own their own hotel or motel" (Ferguson, 2011).

The most crucial for people interested in this business is to know where the best options are. "Some major employers in the industry are Comfort Inn, based in Newark, Delaware; the Hilton Hotels, based in Carolton, Texas; and Mirage Resorts of Las Vegas, which are noted for their quality of management. These companies have properties located nationwide and abroad. Host Marriot Corporation, another international player, offers a fast-track management program for qualified employees and has been known to encourage career advancement for minorities and women" (*Encyclopedia of Careers*, 2003, p. 365). Many factors influence the employment of managers such as weak economic times and the terrorist attacks in the United States of America in 2001. These factors dramatically reduced the number of people willing to travel for business and pleasure. Nevertheless, hotels, resorts, and vocational areas continue to be built, and managers are in need. There is always a need for lodging. "Business travelers are back on the road in 2011, said global professional services firm Deloitte. The company surveyed 1,001 business travelers and found that eighty percent are expecting to take more trips than they did in 2010" (Hertzfeld, 2011, p. 50).

# 5. Interview Data

The ethnographer conducted an interview with an assistance manager of a hotel. The researcher and her informant started their passion for hospitality in the same way, while traveling with their families. When the professional graduated from college, the country was experiencing a recession, and hospitality was the opportunity that he saw. The interviewee started working at one of the biggest hotel chains in the world, The Marriot Corporation, in their time-share division, and he walked his way through into the organization. Presently, in his current job, the informant started in sales marketing, from there, he jumped to the operation side in order to become an assistant manager.

The interviewee explained how a person can jump from being a bellman and speaking limited English to rising quickly and becoming a manager, of course, depending on their efficiency and effectiveness. Working hard and establishing oneself in the work environment yields to mobility and further advancement.

# 6. Conclusion

Lodging establishments offer great opportunities for those who are interested in owning and running their own business. This job is lucrative and helps to create relationships as well. People have to find a job that they enjoy while making a profit from it. Good managers are needed to run almost any kind of establishment, and because hospitality is a very broad field, an employee can expand almost every sector. For guests, it is priceless to receive excellent treatment, consequently managers and owners must train their employees to bring that experience to their guests. Currently, more and more companies are seeking employees with a college degree to hire in their establishments.

People interested in this career have to have proper certifications in order to get a job easily and start building their portfolio. Education is a very important key for advancement in this career. Basically, workers in this field must be ready to provide guests and visitors with gracious customer service at any hour.

In today's technological world, it is crucial for establishments to analyze data while understanding the changes in the global market to ensure customer satisfaction. The researcher is prepared to continue her pursuit of this career. She intends to complete her education, and hopefully, return to her country of origin to work as a manager in a large hotel. The ethnographer's bilingualism will be a real enhancement in the workplace. The researcher is confident that her career goals will come to fruition.

# References

*Encyclopedia of careers and vocational guidance,* Hotel and Motel Managers (12th ed.) (2003), Ferguson Publishing Company.

Hertzfeld, E. (2011, March). Top 100 U.S. Markets leading the recovery. *Hotel Management, 50*(3), 226.

Hospitality Management Program [Brochure (2011)]. Cranford, NJ: Union County College.

Powers, T., & Barrows, C. (2006). *Management in the hospitality industry* (8th ed.). Hoboken, NJ: John Wiley Prentice Hall, Inc.

Riegel, C., & Dallas, M. (1998). *Hospitality and tourism careers.* Saddle River, NJ: Prentice Hall.

Rosenthal, J. (2009, May-June). Medical tourism takes off. *National Geographic Traveler, 26*(4) 10–13.

# Chapter FOUR
# THE ORAL PRESENTATION

 **Oral Presentation**

An oral presentation is a form of assessment that educators frequently use in the classroom. Oral assessments come in a variety of styles, from multimedia projects to group work to speeches. An oral presentation involves explaining something to an audience, usually in an academic environment, but sometimes in a work setting. Educators grade oral presentations based on the quality of the information presented as well as the method of presenting the information.

An individual can give an oral presentation alone or as part of a group. An oral presentation may come with the added component of utilizing some type of technology such as a slide show, video clip, or audio portion as well as a movie trailer. In this case, it might be called a multimedia presentation. Most oral presentations require the presenter to use a combination of spoken words and visual aids in order to present an idea or an explanation to a group of people.

Speaking is one of the three fundamental communication modes. The ability to communicate thorough effective speaking is as important to language skill development as is the ability to write effectively. Competent, effective speaking is perhaps one of the most important skills a person can acquire. Such skills are essential whether we are involved in causal conversation, and explanation of something, presenting a paper to a group of students or colleagues, and attempting to convince someone.

 **Organization of an Oral Presentation**

An oral presentation consists of three main parts: the introduction, body, and conclusion.

### The Introduction

The introduction is a very important component of the presentation. It sets the scene, so to speak, and engages the audience by motivating them to listen by relating the topic to their interests. The simplest introduction may be merely letting the audience know who you are and what your presentation is going to be about. More specific information is obviously needed in the introduction of the presentation. For a specific class assignment, the student would follow the instructor's directives and requirements of the assignment.

A well-crafted introduction should be succinct, although information should be included as well. Therefore, the presenter must give enough background information regarding the topic of the presentation.

The purpose of an introduction is to quickly build rapport with your audience and gain their attention. The presenter wants the audience to be able to easily follow a thought process, leading them into the body of the presentation.

### The Body

The main part of the presentation is the body. The body must expound, explain, and furnish the audience with specific, substantive, concrete information about the topic. All main points must be covered. Use examples and illustrations for information that is difficult for the audience to understand. Do not assume your audience understands what you are presenting. Graphic illustrations and other visual aids not only help to clarify your information, but add color and credibility as well. Visuals are a real enhancement and plus to any presentation.

 ## The Conclusion

The presentation must conclude with a well-planned ending. Do not leave the audience hanging and wondering. The purpose of the conclusion is to wrap up, sum up, and put closure to your presentation. A clear summary of your main points will insure that the audience gets the big picture. It should answer the question, "So what?", telling the audience what was important about the information you conveyed. Utilize the same key words and phrases used in the body and make a fresh, brief, concise summation with strong concluding remarks that reinforce why your information is of value. Do not flounder your exit line. Make a crisp final statement and conclude your presentation on a positive note. Plan and memorize the ending statement, your closing line, and then say it, showing some enthusiasm!

### Deliberation Methods

There are approximately four methods of delivering the content of an oral presentation. The best of these is the extemporaneous method and the worst is the impromptu method. The *extemporaneous* method which is spoken with preparation, but not written out or memorized, and the *impromptu* method which is spoken without preparation or advance practice. In between these two methods are the memorization method and the reading method.

The *extemporaneous* method involves significant effort, but results in a degree of quality that tells your audience that you care about them. This method requires

- A detailed outline of the presentation from the beginning to the end.
- Doing your homework to adhere to assignment guidelines and requirements as well as to fill in your knowledge gaps.
- The use of note cards with key words and phrases to jog your memory on specifics and keep your presentation on track.

The *impromptu* method is characterized by poor organization and incompleteness. It tells the audience that you are indifferent about them. The *memorization* method is risky; you can lose your place or leave something out and, in a panic, you might revert to the impromptu method, resulting in disaster. Finally, the *reading* method might be acceptable if you are presenting a discourse on some technical topic about which you lack expertise. An example could be in presenting a paper at a technical meeting for a colleague who might be ill.

## *Preparation*

Irrespective of the method of delivery, the presenter must consider the following in preparing for the presentation: knowledge of the audience, knowledge of subject, use of time and practice, and personal appearance and grooming. Additionally, the preparation and use of visual aids is an important element of any effective presentation.

- *Knowledge of the audience*: Do not patronize your audience! Neither speak down nor speak up to your audience. How much do they already know about your subject? Know the age level of the audience as well as its members' level of educational sophistication and special interests. Tailor your presentation accordingly.
- *Knowledge of the subject*: Whether you use notes, manuscript, or strictly memory, you must know your subject well.
- *Use of time and practice*: Time limits are to be observed! Even if no time limit is given, you should strive to do justice to your subject in as little time as possible, but not at the price of an incomplete presentation. You must decide which aspects are to be included for additional information and color. *The key to effective and efficient use of time is practice*! Use a stopwatch and rehearse, revise, and continue to rehearse until your presentation is within the target time limit. When you practice, do so in a manner similar to the actual presentation. Once you are well-versed, familiar, and comfortable with the content of your presentation, a good idea would be to practice alone in front of a mirror. Finally, you are ready to invite several family members or friends to listen to your presentation to receive feedback from them.
- *Personal appearance*: Your personal appearance affects your credibility. Informal clothing is rarely appropriate for a professional presentation. Pay significant attention to personal grooming.

## *Stage Fright: Fear and Nervousness*

Even the most polished and professional speakers and actors may suffer a bout of stage fright. While it may not be totally preventable, it is controllable. The best defense against stage fright is preparation and practice. Practice as often as you can in front of others whose opinion you trust to be honest and direct.

Accept nervousness for what it is, a normal, typical part of the preparation for speaking in front of others, and may, believe it or not, be a good thing. It heightens your senses and gets your blood pumping. You will think clearly and move faster. Remember, the more times you do something you fear, the less you will fear it. Good preparation will increase your self-confidence. Once you get going, your good preparation will kick in and before you know it, your presentation will have ended.

## *Language*

It is important to remember that the language used in a presentation reflects upon you as your credibility. Use only professional language appropriate to the audience and the topic. Make sure that correct grammar and word choice are utilized throughout the presentation. Do not use vocabulary that you do not know the meaning of and cannot pronounce correctly.

A typical audience will be comprised of people representing many different social and ethnic groups. Inappropriate remarks may be quite offensive to a diverse group of people. Once you have alienated an audience and you have turned them off, inevitably you have lost them for the remaining presentation.

## *Body Language: Nonverbal Communication*

Eye contact, facial expressions, posture/stance, movements, and gestures are all a part of body language. Body language is a natural part of communication, and the golden rule is to be natural, relaxed, and yourself.

### Positive Body Language

- Have eye contact to keep your audience's attention; try to make eye contact with every person in the room.
- Facial expressions should be natural and friendly. Remember to smile.
- Posture—stand straight, but relaxed. Do not slouch or lean.
- Movement—movement is necessary to indicate a change of focus, and keep the audience's attention.
  - Move forward to emphasize.
  - Move to one side to indicate a transition.
  - Hand and arm movements are necessary as well.
  - Moving about, if not excessive, can accentuate your enthusiasm.
- Gesture—up and down head motion or other movements to indicate importance.
- Poise and Enthusiasm—be well-prepared and strive for control, alert attention, vibrant interest in the topic and an eagerness to communicate.

### Negative Body Language

- Loss of eye contact with your audience as a result of looking and relying heavily on your notes, looking at a screen, at the board, at the floor, or above the heads of your listeners.
- No staring or looking blankly into people's eyes.
- Swaying your body back and forth like a pendulum.
- Turning your back to your audience.
- Nervous habits like taping on a desk or lectern.
- Holding note cards or handouts in hand.
- Putting your hands in your pockets or behind your back.

All this negative body language is a distraction to your audience.

## *Voice Quality and Pronunciation*

Use of voice: Do not speak too softly, too fast, or mumble! Your audience must be able to (a) hear what you say (voice amplitude) and (b) understand what you say (speech, word resolution, and clarity). Use voice emphasis to stress important points. Modulate, enunciate, and use tonal variety. A good speaking voice is not harsh or nasal, but has a pleasing melody. Open your mouth and enunciate clearly. Pay particular attention that you do not garble your words, run words together, or mumble. Have a variety of sounds in your voice. You can give importance to what you are saying by a well-timed pause, lowering your voice, or speaking with emphasis, stressing your points of significance.

## *Pronunciation*

Correct pronunciation is important if one is to be correctly understood. Incorrect pronunciation is perhaps the first cause of communication breakdown. If listeners are not accustomed to the speaker's native language, they will not understand a mispronounced word. Mispronunciation additionally tires the audience's ear and listeners may perhaps even stop trying to understand the speaker if it becomes difficult.

There are two important aspects of pronunciation of individual words: word stress and individual sounds. Make sure you know how to correctly pronounce the key technical words or words that you repeat over and over again in your presentation. Another important point for the presenter to remember is sentence stress that concerns stressing particular words in a sentence usually at regular intervals. English speakers stress words that are important for meaning. Remember clear, correct pronunciation is essential.

Pacing/Use of Time: Without adequate preparation, it is easy to become nervous and rush through a presentation. Instead, use the pacing established during your practices. You planned your presentation, now follow the plan. Do not suddenly decide to "wing it" and go off on some tangent or skip a whole section of your presentation and then find yourself needing to backtrack. Once you do such things, your sense of time and pacing will be severely compromised.

### *Delivering Your Presentation*

People vary in their ability to speak confidently in public, but everyone gets nervous and everyone can learn how to improve their presentation skills by applying a few simple techniques.

The main points to pay attention to in delivery are the quality of your voice, your rapport with the audience, the use of notes, and the use of visual aids.

Voice quality involves attention to volume, speed and fluency, clarity and pronunciation. The quality of your voice in a presentation will improve dramatically if you are able to practice beforehand in a room similar to the one you will be presenting in.

Rapport with the audience involves attention to eye contact, sensitivity to how the audience is responding to your talk, and what you look like from the point of view of the audience. These can be improved by practice in front of one or two friends or videotaping your practice.

### *Effective Use of Note Cards*

Good speakers vary a great deal in their use of notes. Some do not use notes at all and some write out their talk in great detail. If you are not an experienced speaker, it is not a good idea to speak without notes because you will soon lose your thread. You should also avoid reading a prepared text aloud or memorizing your speech, as this will be boring.

The best solution may be to use notes with headings and points to be covered. You may also want to write down key sentences. Notes must be placed on index cards. Some speakers use overhead transparencies as notes. The trick in using notes is to avoid shifting your attention from the audience for too long. Your notes should always be written large enough for you to see.

### *Delivery of Content: Things to Remember*

- Begin your presentation by telling your audience what your topic is and what you will be covering. Audiences like to have a guidepost.
- Avoid reading your remarks.
- Dress neatly and appropriately. The rule of thumb is to dress one level nicer than the audience will be dressed.

- Speak in a clear, audible voice, loud enough to be clearly heard in the back row. *Never, ever mumble.*
- Stand up straight, do not slouch or drape yourself around the podium. Do not be afraid to move around the room somewhat, moving around is good; it causes the audience to pay attention.
- Do not stand like a stiff board.
- Do not rock back and forth on your heels, tap a pencil, or play with a pencil or pointer; do not do things that will distract from your content.
- Never apologize to your audience for the state of your knowledge or your degree of preparation. The audience wants to have confidence in you. You are the authority; do nothing to undermine your authority.
- Never mention anything that could have been in your talk, but wasn't.
- Make frequent eye contact with the audience. Really look at the audience as you talk to them. Engaging them directly with your eyes transfers a bit of your energy to them and keeps them focused on your content. Making eye contact says that you are in charge of the room and of your presentation. This is what you want. Work the room with your eyes, and make each person feel important.
- If you use slides or PowerPoint, avoid the tendency to speak to the screen instead of to the audience. Be so familiar with your visual aids that the only reason you look at them is to point something out.
- Never turn your back on the audience and try to avoid walking in front of the projector.
- Adhere strictly to your time limit. Organize your main points and rate of speech so that you speak for your required time. You will be surprised how quickly the time goes.
- At the conclusion of your presentation, ask for questions. Encourage questions with your eyes and your body language. Respond to questions politely, good-humoredly, and briefly. Take a quick moment to compose your thoughts before responding if you need to.

## *An Effective Oral Presentation*

- **Be prepared:** Research your subject to ensure that you are knowledgeable. Practice your presentation until you feel comfortable. Make sure you can present your information within whatever time limits you will have. Anticipate questions you may be asked and prepare answers to these.
- **Know your audience:** Tailor your presentation to your audience's level of knowledge about the subject of your presentation, what they need to know, and their interests.
- **Be positive:** Make it clear that you are knowledgeable and enthusiastic about your subject.
- **Do not read your presentation:** Talk to your audience. Use your notes as prompts as needed.
- **Use visual aids:** Supplement what you say with visual aids such as handouts, charts, transparencies, and slides. Make sure that everyone can easily see the visual aids. Do not use visual aids that are so complex that the audience will spend their time trying to read them instead of listening to you. Visual aids are supplements to what you say, not replacements for what you say.
- **Maintain eye contact:** Shift your eye contact around the room so that everyone feels that you are talking to them.
- **Actively involve your audience:** People can only listen so long without their attention wandering. Making your presentation interesting will help you to capture and keep your audience's attention for awhile, but you must do more. Build in some simple and quick activities for your audience so that they are actively involved in your presentation. Ask questions that you are confident your audience will be able to answer.

- **Use your voice effectively:** Vary the tone of your voice and be careful not to talk too quickly.
- **End on a high note:** Leave your audience feeling upbeat about what they have just heard.

### *The Audience Role*

Presentations involve both a speaker and the audience. People in the audience play a role in how well a presentation goes. People in the audience have an obligation to:

- Do not be late
- Listen politely
- Have eye contact with the speaker
- Do not talk with others in the audience
- Control negative facial expressions
- Control bored body language
- Do not put your head down on the desk or tilt your head back to sleep
- Do not constantly check your watch or the clock on the wall
- Expect a Question and Answer period to be part of the presentation
- Participate in Question and Answer period either by listening or by posing a question
- Prepare to remain attentive throughout the Question and Answer
- Never leave the room
- Do not look over your own presentation notes if you are also giving a presentation

### *Visual Aids*

Visual aids can either make or break your presentation. They (maps, photos, film clips, graphs, diagrams, and charts) can enhance a presentation. They can help you keep your presentation on track as well as assist your audience in following your main thoughts. They may be used as a guide in helping you to remember main points and their order. Visuals can either include a series of slides or transparencies or the use of a computer presentation graphics application such as PowerPoint, enabling presenters to explain each visual as their presentation progresses. Remember, a good graphic can have a value equivalent to over 100 words.

Practice your presentation with the visual aids you will actually use during the presentation. Do not read from your slides to your audience, but use your visuals to guide and focus your audience's attention, reinforce your main points, and provide detail.

Visual aids can help to make your presentation livelier. They can also help the audience to follow your presentation and help you to present information that would be difficult to follow through speech alone.

The two most common forms of visual aids are overhead transparencies (OHTs) and computer slide shows (e.g., PowerPoint). Objects that can be displayed or passed around the audience can also be very effective and often help to relax the audience.

### PowerPoint Slides

Microsoft PowerPoint slides are additions to a presentation in an effort to add to, not be the focus of, the presentation.

Keep slides simple and uncluttered. Use color and contrast for emphasis, but use them in moderation. Use a font large enough to be seen from the back of the room.

### *Equipment Advice*

- Work out details with equipment before the day of your presentation.
- Know how to operate the equipment you choose to use.
- If you are using PowerPoint, have a backup copy on a disk.
- Consider making OHTs of your PowerPoint in case there is a problem with the technology.
- Consider making print duplicates of your slides or transparencies in case there is a problem with electricity or bulbs.
- Do not expect a network connection to work when you need it. Have any Web sites you hope to show available as offline copies on a disk. Work offline whenever possible to avoid slow network response.

### *Handouts*

Handouts provide structure. This can provide supplemental material, references, a glossary of terms, and serve as a record of the presentation. The handout should be attractively laid out and inviting to read.

Some speakers give printed handouts to the audience to follow as they speak. Others prefer to give their handouts at the end of the talk because they can distract the audience from the presentation.

 **NOTE:** Any visual aids made by the presenter must be large enough to be seen by the audience. Graphs, diagrams, charts, photos, and illustrations must have minimal text. Key words and phrases are sufficient, and must be in large lettering, enabling everyone in the audience to readily see.

### *Career Oral Presentation*

The career oral presentation is the final step in the completion of the career research project. This component of the assignment is by far the easiest to execute. The researcher has completed both the ethnographic interview as well as the career research paper. It is the appropriate time for the ethnographer to share the information acquired from these sources with their classmates and professor.

Extracting significant, interesting, contradictory, and striking points from the interview and research paper and sharing what they have learned in an oral presentation is a gratifying experience for the ethnographer. Additionally, the audience learns a wealth of interesting information from the presenters. Students who share a specific career choice have the option of conducting the interview together with a professional, of sharing sources for their research papers, and of collaboratively presenting their findings in the oral presentation.

 ## Organization of Career Oral Presentation

### *Outline to Your Presentation*

#### Introduction

- Tell your audience who you are.
- Give some background information about yourself.
- What is your career choice?
- How did you get interested in this career?

#### Body

- Highlight the most significant, interesting, striking, and possibly contradictory points of the ethnographic interview.
- Highlight the most significant, interesting, striking and possibly contradictory points of the research paper.

- Are there any contradictions between the interview data and research data?
- Evaluation of the Career Research Project. Evaluate the components of the project: the ethnographic interview and the research paper.

  - Do you have a preference?
  - Did you prefer conducting the interview or writing the paper?
  - Explain your preference

### Conclusion

- Tell your audience your career goals and aspirations.
- Have you changed your mind about your career choice as a result of this project? Or, have you confirmed that your career choice is what you really want after completion of this project?
- What are your present plans?
- What are your future plans?

 ## Oral Presentation

### *The Student Checklist*
### Introduction

- Career choice
- Interest in career

### Body

1. Highlight major points of the ethnographic interview.
2. Highlight major points of the research paper.
3. Which did you prefer? Research paper or interview? Why?

### Conclusion

- Career goals/aspirations
- Today—future

---

 **NOTE:**
- Your oral presentation should be approximately 5–10 minutes in length.
- Use index cards for notes (if needed)
- Visual aids
- Voice quality
- Eye contact
- Deliberation of speech—The student will determine the method of delivery.

---

# Chapter FIVE
## OUTCOMES

 **Outcomes**

Learning outcomes are statements that describe significant and essential learning that learners have achieved. Learning outcomes identify what the learner will know and be able to do by the end of a course or program.

The learning outcomes approach to education means basing program and curriculum design, content, delivery, and assessment on an analysis of the integrated knowledge, skills needed by both students and society. In this outcomes-based approach to education, the ability to demonstrate learning is the key point.

What are the differences between objectives and outcomes? Objectives are *intended* results or consequences of instruction, curricula, programs, or activities. Outcomes are *achieved* results or consequences of what was learned. The outcomes are the evidence that learning took place. Objectives are focused on specific types of performances that students are expected to demonstrate at the end of instruction. Objectives are often written more in terms of teaching intentions and typically indicate the subject content that the educator intends to cover. Learning outcomes, on the other hand, are more student-centered and describe what it is that the learner should learn.

Learning outcomes are statements that specify what learners will know or be able to do as a result of a learning activity. Outcomes are more precise, specific, and measurable than goals. There can be more than one outcome related to each goal and a particular learning outcome can support more than one goal.

The career research project has been included in the author's freshman composition writing courses for many years. The diverse student population who are required to take this class is an inclusion of Native Americans and second language learners from over 80 countries of the world. The implementation and execution of this project takes approximately 1 month from beginning to completion. The students are given a satisfactory timeline to complete the three necessary components of ethnographic interview, research paper, and oral presentation of the project.

The intended results stated in objectives at the completion of Chapter 1: Overview have successfully been achieved. In a longitudinal study of 20 plus years, the results reported are positive. Over 95% of students who have completed the career research project over these years have earned a grade of C or higher on the ethnographic interview, research paper, and oral presentation.

The reported outcomes are successful. The students *are able* to:

- Write a research paper using APA style.
- Independently revise and edit their writing.
- Effectively paraphrase and avoid plagiarizing.
- Independently incorporate primary and secondary sources to support and refute ideas.
- Hone public speaking skills, including using a clear voice and timing a speech.
- Hone multimedia skills in preparation of visual and auditory aids for an oral presentation.
- Acquire teaching skills in the preparation of material to demonstrate to an audience in an oral presentation.

### *Student Commentary*

The following student statements are confirmation of positive outcomes. These statements were made during career oral presentations and told directly to the professor.

- "Your demand for APA format papers has truly helped me in my nursing program."
- "I was skeptical of the Career Research Project we had to do, the interview was gut wrenching. I never thought it would be so helpful to do the interview."
- "The style you wanted the interview to be conducted in has helped me in several ways. You wanted open-ended questions, and the questions were based on the information already provided. This skill has helped me when assessing patients, because I retrieve more information which is much needed when clustering data for a nursing diagnosis."
- "My clinical communication skills are amazing as a result of the ethnographic interview."
- "Hopefully, future nursing students/health care majors will take into consideration the beneficial aspects of the career research project."
- "I loved conducting this interview. My informant asked if I would like an apprenticeship in his company this summer."
- "I am so excited! Six months after conducting my ethnographic interview with a dentist, he called and said he would train me to be his assistant. His office is far away, but I have accepted the job."
- "The politician I interviewed in Newark recommended me for a job in Washington, D.C., and I'm going. I can't wait!"
- "The informant started asking me questions at the end of the interview. I think he liked me, and offered me a job in his language school to help out. It is a plus that I am bilingual."
- "The hotel manager asked me to work in the hotel at the desk. I'm quitting my babysitting job, and starting next week. I am so happy for this opportunity."
- "I was offered a job at Johnson and Johnson* and the company will pay my tuition."

### *Informant Commentary*

The following informant statements are confirmation of positive outcomes. These verbatim comments were extracted from student ethnographic interviews during the professor's evaluation of the recordings.

- "When are you completing school and earning your degree? Are you almost finished? Here is my business card. Come back once you have earned your degree. I will have a job for you in my company."
- "Are you interested in an apprenticeship for the summer? We cannot pay you, but you will learn a great deal about the career."
- "I am very impressed with you. We need good people like you in the field."

- "I do not recommend this career. It is a lot of hard work, and after many years of working as a mechanic, my body feels it."
- "We need good male nurses. Hurry up and get your degree. There are not enough male nurses in the field."
- "There are many risks in the nursing field, but the rewards outnumber the risks you take."
- "I can tell you have what it takes to be a great firefighter."
- "Are you interested in working at my law firm at the desk? I can pay you fifteen dollars an hour."
- "You have asked some very good questions about the career. You seem to already know a great deal about the profession."
- "As a student interested in becoming a stockbroker, I recommend you subscribe to this journal. It is considered "The Bible" in the stock market field. It is essential for you to be familiar with it now."

The career research project has continued to serve the students in a positive and meaningful way. As a result of this project, students have either enthusiastically confirmed their career choices that they were indecisive about initially, or have changed their majors in pursuit of a different career path. Networking has been an additional plus of this project. Students have made important, meaningful professional connections.

Finally, the positive and successful outcomes of the career research project support its perpetuation and continuation. The student benefits are numerous yielding gratification to both the student and educator. The author stands in firm support of this exceptional project.

*Appendix*

# EVALUATION FORMS
## (RUBRICS)

# Interview

| | Excellent | Very Good | Good | Fair | Poor |
|---|---|---|---|---|---|
| A. Choice of Informant | 5 | 4 | 3 | 2 | 1 |
| B. Appropriate Introduction (Stroking) | 5 | 4 | 3 | 2 | 1 |
| C. Body<br>Types of Questions: Descriptive, Structural, Contrast, and Clarification | 5 | 4 | 3 | 2 | 1 |
| Were your questions based on your informant's responses? | 5 | 4 | 3 | 2 | 1 |
| Were your questions based on your research data? | 5 | 4 | 3 | 2 | 1 |
| D. Expression of Cultural Ignorance and Cultural Interest | 5 | 4 | 3 | 2 | 1 |
| E. Is your interview unstructured, informal, a friendly conversation, and a free elicitation of verbal exchange? | 5 | 4 | 3 | 2 | 1 |
| F. Conclusion (Stroking)<br>Was the appropriate question asked after pausing occurred? | 5 | 4 | 3 | 2 | 1 |

Professor's Overall Comments:          Grade

# Research Paper

| | Excellent | Very Good | Good | Fair | Poor |
|---|---|---|---|---|---|
| A. Components of Paper: Are all sections included? Is the paper substantive and informative? | 5 | 4 | 3 | 2 | 1 |
| B. Title Page/Table of Contents | 5 | 4 | 3 | 2 | 1 |
| C. Introduction and Conclusion | 5 | 4 | 3 | 2 | 1 |
| D. Interview Data Participant Observation | 5 | 4 | 3 | 2 | 1 |
| E. APA Format Is APA format followed throughout the paper? | 5 | 4 | 3 | 2 | 1 |
| F. APA Format for In-text Citations Direct and Indirect Variations | 5 | 4 | 3 | 2 | 1 |
| G. APA Format for References | 5 | 4 | 3 | 2 | 1 |
| H. Mechanics: Have you proofread, revised, and edited your paper? | 5 | 4 | 3 | 2 | 1 |

Professor's Overall Comments:        Grade

# Oral Presentation

| | Excellent | Very Good | Good | Fair | Poor |
|---|---|---|---|---|---|
| A. Stance: Did you have good posture and stand quietly or did you fidget? | 5 | 4 | 3 | 2 | 1 |
| B. Gestures: Did you use movement in such a way as to enhance the presentation? | 5 | 4 | 3 | 2 | 1 |
| C. Eye Contact: Did you look at the audience, or somewhere else? | 5 | 4 | 3 | 2 | 1 |
| D. Voice/Pronounciation/Enunciation/Audibility/ Clarity | 5 | 4 | 3 | 2 | 1 |
| Rate: Too fast, too slow, or just right? | 5 | 4 | 3 | 2 | 1 |
| Volume: Too loud, too soft, or just right? | 5 | 4 | 3 | 2 | 1 |
| Enunciation: Did you pronounce each word clearly, or did you mumble? | 5 | 4 | 3 | 2 | 1 |
| Expression: Did you vary the tone of your voice in order to make the meaning clear, or were you monotone? Enthusiasm and vocal variation | 5 | 4 | 3 | 2 | 1 |
| E. Phrasing: Vocabulary and use of appropriate words Did you group the words together in a meaningful way and use the punctuation as a guide for pausing or were you unfamiliar with your content and had many pauses in your speaking? | 5 | 4 | 3 | 2 | 1 |
| F. Preparation: Did you practice enough to really learn the important points? | 5 | 4 | 3 | 2 | 1 |
| G. Content and Organization: Did you have an evident introduction, body, and conclusion, including pertinent information, with preparation and knowledge of materials? | 5 | 4 | 3 | 2 | 1 |
| H. Visual Aids: appropriateness and effectiveness | 5 | 4 | 3 | 2 | 1 |

Professor's Overall Comments:                    Grade